CAMBRIDGE LIBRARY COLLECTION

Books of enduring scholarly value

Religion

For centuries, scripture and theology were the focus of prodigious amounts of scholarship and publishing, dominated in the English-speaking world by the work of Protestant Christians. Enlightenment philosophy and science, anthropology, ethnology and the colonial experience all brought new perspectives, lively debates and heated controversies to the study of religion and its role in the world, many of which continue to this day. This series explores the editing and interpretation of religious texts, the history of religious ideas and institutions, and not least the encounter between religion and science.

The Forty Martyrs of the Sinai Desert

The twin sisters Agnes Lewis (1843–1926) and Margaret Gibson (1843–1920) were pioneering biblical scholars who became experts in a number of ancient languages. Travelling widely in the Middle East, they made several significant discoveries, including one of the earliest manuscripts of the four gospels in Syriac, a dialect of Aramaic, the language probably spoken by Jesus himself. Originally published in the Horae Semitica series, this fascicule features a text in Arabic and Syriac which tells the story of the massacre of monks at the Sinai monastery in the fourth century. It is a mournful account of extreme suffering for the Christian faith. Edited and translated by Agnes Lewis, the volume also includes the tale of Eulogius, a hubristic stone-cutter. Rewarded by God for his charity, Eulogius was corrupted by wealth, returning to his humble position a broken man. Both documents are of great historical and linguistic interest.

Cambridge University Press has long been a pioneer in the reissuing of out-of-print titles from its own backlist, producing digital reprints of books that are still sought after by scholars and students but could not be reprinted economically using traditional technology. The Cambridge Library Collection extends this activity to a wider range of books which are still of importance to researchers and professionals, either for the source material they contain, or as landmarks in the history of their academic discipline.

Drawing from the world-renowned collections in the Cambridge University Library, and guided by the advice of experts in each subject area, Cambridge University Press is using state-of-the-art scanning machines in its own Printing House to capture the content of each book selected for inclusion. The files are processed to give a consistently clear, crisp image, and the books finished to the high quality standard for which the Press is recognised around the world. The latest print-on-demand technology ensures that the books will remain available indefinitely, and that orders for single or multiple copies can quickly be supplied.

The Cambridge Library Collection will bring back to life books of enduring scholarly value (including out-of-copyright works originally issued by other publishers) across a wide range of disciplines in the humanities and social sciences and in science and technology.

The Forty Martyrs of the Sinai Desert

And the Story of Eulogios, from a Palestinian Syriac and Arabic Palimpsest

Edited by Agnes Smith Lewis

CAMBRIDGE UNIVERSITY PRESS

CAMBRIDGE UNIVERSITY PRESS

Cambridge, New York, Melbourne, Madrid, Cape Town,
Singapore, São Paolo, Delhi, Tokyo, Mexico City

Published in the United States of America by Cambridge University Press, New York

www.cambridge.org
Information on this title: www.cambridge.org/9781108019088

This edition first published 1912
This digitally printed version 2011

ISBN 978-1-108-01908-8 Paperback

THE FORTY MARTYRS OF THE SINAI DESERT

AND THE STORY OF EULOGIOS

CAMBRIDGE UNIVERSITY PRESS
London: FETTER LANE, E.C.
C. F. CLAY, Manager

Edinburgh: 100, PRINCES STREET
Berlin: A. ASHER AND CO.
Leipzig: F. A. BROCKHAUS
New York: G. P. PUTNAM'S SONS
Bombay and Calcutta: MACMILLAN AND CO., Ltd.

Ruined Monastery of the Araba'în or Forty Martyrs
on Mount Sinai

HORAE SEMITICAE No. IX

THE FORTY MARTYRS OF THE SINAI DESERT

AND THE STORY OF EULOGIOS

FROM A PALESTINIAN SYRIAC AND ARABIC PALIMPSEST

TRANSCRIBED BY

AGNES SMITH LEWIS, M.R.A.S.

HON. D.D. (HEIDELBERG); LITT.D. (DUBLIN); LL.D. (ST ANDREWS);
PH.D. (HALLE-WITTENBERG)

CAMBRIDGE
AT THE UNIVERSITY PRESS
1912

Cambridge:
PRINTED BY JOHN CLAY, M.A.
AT THE UNIVERSITY PRESS

Τοῖς ἐν τῷ Σινᾷ Ὄρῳ Ἱερομοναχοῖς

τοῖς τῶν ἐν Ῥαϊθᾷ Μαρτύρων Διαδόχοις

τὸ τῆς ἱστορίας ἐκείνων ἀντίγραφον συριστὶ μεταφρασθὲν

Ἀφιερόει

AGNES SMITH LEWIS

PREFACE

THIS little volume contains two narratives, one a plain unvarnished tale, which is not without human interest as a record of suffering for the Christian faith; the other partaking somewhat of the character of a romance, which, but for its religious setting, would have done no discredit to a volume of the Thousand and One Nights. The chief value of both, as I am told by Dr Friedrich Schulthess, is a linguistic one; for they are the only non-biblical documents of any length which have come down to us in the Palestinian-Syriac dialect.

I have to thank Dr Nestle for his unfailing kindness in reading my proof-sheets, and for more than one wise suggestion; Dr Friedrich Schulthess, for bringing his unrivalled experience in this Palestinian dialect, and his keen powers of insight, to bear on puzzling questions; and my dear sister, Mrs Margaret Dunlop Gibson, for clearing away unsuspected misprints; also the Reader and Printers of the Cambridge University Press, for their careful work.

AGNES SMITH LEWIS.

CASTLE-BRAE,
CAMBRIDGE,
December, 1911.

CONTENTS

LIST OF ILLUSTRATIONS

INTRODUCTION

THE two stories in this volume are taken from a manuscript which I purchased in Egypt in the month of April 1906 along with the more important one which I have edited under the title of Codex Climaci Rescriptus, as No. VIII of this series. Both MSS. are palimpsests, and the under-script of both is in that dialect of Syriac which, as Bar Hebraeus tells us, was called by the people who spoke it Palestinian, and which was the mother tongue of our Lord, and was doubtless identical with the Galilean speech which "bewrayed" St Peter to the company in the court of Caiaphas, in that terrible hour when he fell, through fear, into the greatest sin of his life. In neither MS. has the date been preserved, for in both the final leaves have been lost. Only from the characteristics of the later writing can we tell at what period the earlier one came into being. The Edessene Syriac text which overlies the Palestinian one of Codex Climaci is assigned, with very good reason, by Mr A. G. Ellis and Rev. G. Margoliouth of the British Museum, to the ninth century A.D. Its under-script cannot be much later than the sixth century A.D., and it is therefore the earliest document of any length in the dialect, as it is also the only one which gives us a continuous text of some of the Pauline Epistles.

The present text is, we think, a century later, and its upper-script is Arabic, not Syriac. The handwriting is a somewhat rare specimen of Christian Arabic, which is easily assigned to the beginning of the tenth century. Its characteristics will easily be understood by a study of the facsimile which I have given (see page 53). It is by no means easy to read, for in addition to its Cufic *sads* and *dads*, it has a د, a ذ, a ط, and a ظ furnished with a tall limb something like that of an initial ك, for which letter the unwary might mistake them. It is also very closely written; for evidently in the tenth century vellum had become scarce. I have not been able to identify it in any way. I can only see that it is a theological treatise; the record of a dispute between a Christian and an unbeliever. Like most literature of its class and period, it contains numerous mistakes in spelling and grammar. There are also many erasures, some of which will be observed in the facsimile. The reason of these, so far as I can judge, is that the unbeliever was often very irreverent in speaking of the Lord Jesus Christ; and possibly the Christian repeated some of his phrases.

If we are satisfied that this Arabic upper-script should be assigned to the early part of the tenth century, we may easily guess that the under one belongs to the seventh. By no ingenuity can we place it earlier, for the second story contains a definite and well-known historical date, on page 76 of this book, that of the death of the Emperor Justinus I and the accession of Justinianus I, his nephew and adopted son, both of these events taking place in A.D. 527.

I therefore think that the text of this MS. must have been written a little more than 100 years after the events which it records. The massacre of the monks at Raïtho might well happen in the first fervour of the Saracenic tribes, after their conversion to Islâm; and though the tale of Eulogios is somewhat fanciful, I see no reason to doubt that it is probably founded on an actual occurrence, and may be looked on in the light of a historical romance, where the supernatural has been brought in to explain the sudden rise and equally sudden fall of a man who meant well, but whose head was turned by the pride and splendour of the position to which his wealth had enabled him to climb. If he really found a hidden treasure, it may possibly have been a store of turquoises, left near Sarâbit el Kadim by some Egyptian miner, or the hoard of a pilgrim who had lost his clue to its hiding-place; like the owner of a small store of copper coins found near the top of Jebel Musa, and now in my own possession.

When the "Martyrs of Raïthō" and the story of the "Pledge of Eulogios" were written, vellum was plentiful. The leaves of the original MS. measure 9 inches by 8, i.e. 22½ centimetres by 20, yet it contains on a page only two columns of 22 short lines each; as the lines have often only one word, or at the most two in them, this gives about 63 words to a page.

The tenth century scribe, who wrote a Christian work in Arabic, could not afford to spread out his text in this fashion. He began by folding his leaves, so as to turn each into two conjugates, and on each of these he wrote about 34 lines of Arabic in one column, as closely as he possibly could. The result is that his pages are only half the size of the original ones, and measure 8 inches by nearly 4½, or 20 centimetres by 11. Each line contains from 7 to 9 words, and each page approximately 270 words. Thus 540 Arabic words overlie 63 of the original Syriac.

The story of the massacre at Raïthō was recorded by Ammonius. It can lay no claim to any grace of style, and is the work of a contemporary chronicler rather than that of a historian. Its Greek and Latin text will be found in the pages of Combefis; but these, as well as the Syriac, were translated by Ammonius himself from the Egyptian or Coptic.

The tale of Eulogios cannot, of course, be literally true; yet it contains a practical lesson. I myself have known persons in real life who were most estimable and useful when in a humble station, but who, when raised to a position of affluence by some injudicious friend, displayed qualities that were not so admirable.

This palimpsest MS. has incidentally served a purpose for which it was not intended. Like the Pyramids, it has been the age-long tomb of a once living thing. I was obliged to cut all the cords which bound its quires together. While doing so I found, embedded between two of its leaves, a large moth, which must have crept in when the book was open, and been squeezed to death perhaps nearly 1000 years ago. I showed it to Dr A. E. Shipley, now Master of Christ's College, Cambridge, who told me that it is a species of Polyodon, one of the common noctuid moths, and that Dr Sharp thinks it may possibly have been in the MS. since the tenth century. Its colouring was exactly that of the leaves which had so long enshrouded it; and I have adorned my title-page with its portrait.

There is little to say about the quires, for they belong to the later script only. They all consist of 8 leaves, for though the second appears to have 6 and the fourth 2, I suspect that the man from whom I bought it, disarranged them by making a slit in the conjugate pair whose leaves I have mistakenly numbered 23 and 24. He cut them for the purpose of sending them about as specimens; and they contain the story of Eulogios finding the treasure. The vellum is fine but strong.

In compiling a Glossary of the new words and forms which appear in Codex Climaci, and in this text (Horae Semiticae VIII and IX), I take the opportunity both of accepting a few emendations suggested by Dr Hugo Duensing, and of justifying myself in regard to some words which he has declared to be errors in my transcription[1]. Critics, it will be observed, are quite as liable to make mistakes as editors are; and this frequently happens when they have given too hasty a consideration to a subject. The occurrence of several passages, however, where Dr Duensing has been able to point out an undoubted slip in the text of the MS., shows that Codex Climaci is not the autograph of the translator, but is a copy of his work; and that we must place the date of the Palestinian version much earlier than the sixth century, to which period Dr Burkitt, with no sufficient proof, has assigned it. Dr Nöldeke's hypothesis, that it belongs to the fourth century, is nearer the truth, though we cannot say that it is absolutely certain.

[1] These are marked in the Glossary by the sign ♣

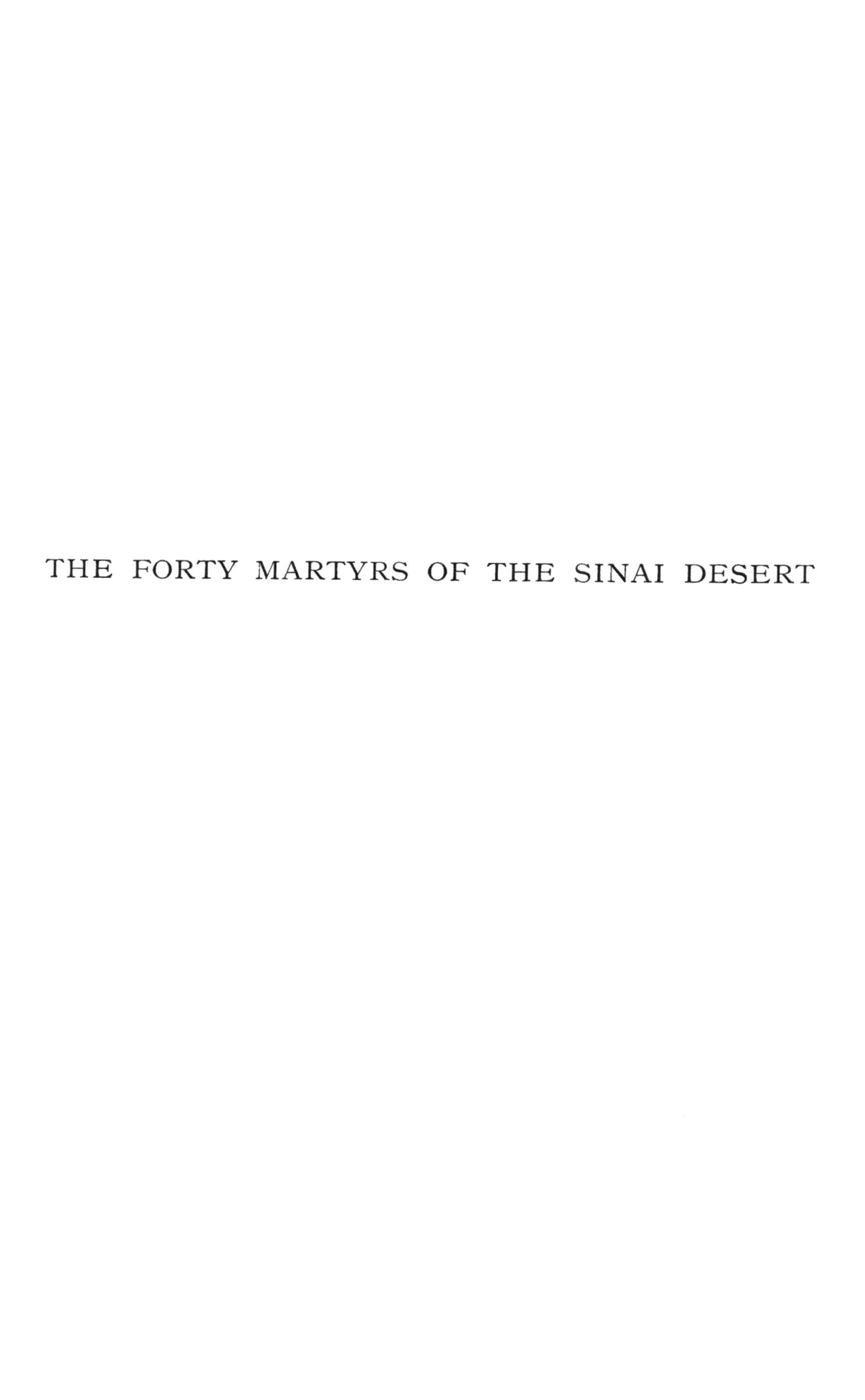

THE FORTY MARTYRS OF THE SINAI DESERT

PART I

THE FORTY MARTYRS OF THE SINAI DESERT

[THE narratives of Ammonius the monk, concerning the Holy Fathers who perished in a raid of the Barbarians on Mount Sinai, and Raïtho.

It occurred to my mind, once upon a time, while I was sitting in my humble cell not far from Alexandria, in a place called Canopus, that I would undertake a journey into Palestine. For in the first place, that I might see with my eyes, but not bear the vexations, and the danger, which was daily caused to the faithful by the cruelty of wicked tyrants. For certainly our very holy President Peter, when he sought hiding-places from place to place, and procured safety by flight, obtained no direct remission, nothing secure for the feeding of his flock. Besides these things, I was also inspired by a desire to survey the venerable places, and a pious zeal for adoring the Holy Sepulchre, with the vivifying and inviolate Resurrection; also the other holy places, in which our Lord Jesus the Christ walked about, and effected His tremendous mysteries.

Having turned a little aside to adore the holy places, and having been refreshed in mind by all the works of God, and having fulfilled [my] vows, that I might profit by the holy places.]

(f. 58a) I was held worthy to worship also in the holy place of the p. 2
Almighty. But I devoted[1] myself to the desert, with people who feared God, (f. 63 b) who were going thither to pray. Now we arrived there, by the grace of God, in eighteen days. And when I had prayed, I remained there for a few (f. 58a) days. And I enjoyed the peculiar polity of the holy fathers who [were] there; for I went with them to their cells, because of the welfare (f. 63b) of my soul. For all the week[2] they sit in silence, but on the evening
of the sabbath they were assembled in the church, (f. 58 b) accomplishing p. 3
the service[3] of the first day of the week. And in the morning they took the Holy Mysteries; the Body and the Blood of the Lord Jesus. And in silence they went every man (f. 63 a) to his cell. But their aspect and also their discipline was like that of angels. Their bodies were all of them very pallid,

[1] Literally "gave." [2] Or "sabbath." [3] Literally "Canon"

as one (f. 58 b) might say, incorporeal; for they possessed nothing for the wants of the body; no wine, no oil, no bread was to be found at once [belonging] to them, except (f. 63 a) a few dates, and what was suitable for them. But for strangers
p. 4 who come to pray there, (f. 30 a) a little bread was placed there beside the Governor of the place.

And after a few days suddenly many of the Saracens fell upon us; because at that (f. 27 b) time the king of the Saracens had died, he who was the guardian of the desert. And they killed those of the fathers who were found (f. 30a) in distant cells. But those who were dwelling in places near, when they heard (the commotion) fled to a certain fortress in the neighbourhood, (together) with the Governor of the place, (f. 27 b) he whose name was Dulos; for he was in truth a servant of God; for great was his long-suffering and humility; and many there were
p. 5 (f. 30 b) who called him Moses the servant of God. And they killed in Geth-rabbi all those whom they found there; and in Choreb; and people in Codar; and all those (f. 27 a) whom they found near to the Holy Mountain. And they came also as far as ourselves; and were also nearly killing us; for no (f. 30 b) man stood up against them; except the merciful God; He who stretched out His hand in conjunction with those who call upon Him from their whole heart. And He commanded (f. 27 a) and a flame of fire was seen on the summit of the Holy Mount, and it was a wonder; and all the mountain [was smoking, and the fire bursting out up to the sky. All being seized with terror, we became insensible through the fear of the vision. And falling on our faces, we worshipped God, and supplicated that He would carry us over the present necessity, which lay heavy on us, to a prosperous issue. Nay, even the Barbarians also, terrified by this new and unwonted sight, by a sudden impulse took to flight, many [of them] even leaving [their] arms with [their] camels, nor did they brook a moment's[1] delay. And now when we saw that they were scattered in flight, we poured out our thanks, and glorified God, who had not over-looked His suppliants, until the end. But descending from Tôr, we searched (to find out) which of the Fathers had been killed, and where. We found the names of the slain to be thirty-eight, some with different limbs, and differing wounds, cut and deformed. The manner in which they had been killed, no one will be able hereafter to tell, as no one saw how the massacre happened. We found twelve of these saints in the Monastery of Geth-rabbi, but several in quite other places. Isaiah and
p. 6 Saba badly wounded (f. 55 a)] and still breathing. And we were in great affliction. We buried also those who had been slain. And we attended to those brethren who were ill.

For who (f. 50 b) even if his heart were of stone, would not weep and lament

[1] Literally "the delay of a moment of an hour," "horae momentum moram."

for the holy martyrs who had grown old in the garb of Christians, (f. 55 a)
flung upon the ground in merciless suffering; each one of them struck down,
one with his head cut off, and another cleft in twain; and another with his head
split in two. What can I (f. 50 b) say about the number of merciless blows
which struck the saints who were killed limb by limb, and were flung upon the
ground? (f. 55 b) For no word can tell all that our eyes saw, on the bodies p. 7
of these saints; Father Isaiah died after a day (had passed). (f. 50 a) Also
Saba himself was thrown down in the hope of life; because his wound
was not very bad, and he was (f. 55 b) praising God greatly for what had
happened. But he was sad that he had not become worthy of the end of the
saints who had been slain. And he wept and said, "Woe (f. 50 a) is me, the
miserable one! that I did not become worthy of the number of the holy
fathers who have been slain for the sake of the Christ, (f. 76 a) who was
cut off at the eleventh hour; he who saw the haven of the kingdom, and p. 8
did not enter it." And he said this with weeping, and begged from God, and
said: "Thou art He (f. 79 b) alone [who] hast loved men. Do not separate
me from the holy fathers those who have been slain for Thy name, (f. 76 a)
but let the number of the Forty Martyrs be fulfilled in me. Yea, Lord Jesus,
Son of the Living God, have mercy upon me, because Thou knowest I have
cleaved unto Thee from my youth, (f. 79 b) and I have loved Thee and have
longed for Thee. I am sinful and polluted."

And when he had said these things with a wise and true thought, (f. 76 b)
he surrendered his spirit to God, on the fourth day after all the holy men. p. 9
And while we were in lamentation and in tears, a certain Saracen came,
(f. 79 a) and said unto us, that the monks, after they had dwelt amongst the
Barbarians, went their way to the place that is called Raïtho, and were slain
(f. 76 b) by the Barbarians. The dwelling was distant from us a march of
two days, which is on the shore of the Red Sea, where Moses (f. 79 a)
and the people of God encamped when they had come out of Egypt. There
are those twelve springs of water and the palm-trees which are written [about]
(f. 19 a) in the Exodus, "seventy palm-trees, and twelve springs," which have p. 10
increased very greatly in numbers. And this Saracen related to us about
the slain (f. 18 b) of Raïtho. We asked him to tell us on what day they were
slain; and how many were slain. And he said unto us, "I (f. 19 a) know
not, but I have heard the report from others, of those who dwelt here that
they were all slain." And while he was still telling us, others came (f. 18 b)
[and] said that truly it had happened. And then after a few days, a monk came
to us from the monks who were dwelling there, (f. 19 b) and he said unto us,
"Here on Mount Sinai I wish to dwell, because the desert in which I dwell p. 11
has been laid waste by the Barbarians." And when Father (f. 18 a) Dulos, the

Governor of the place, heard [it] he received him with joy. And he asked him
to make known to him the truth of what happened to the saints (f. 19 b) who
were slain at Raïtho; and of how he escaped from the Barbarians; and what
was their polity; and also about their discipline.

Beginning of a chapter. (f. 18 a) And when he mentioned the discipline
of the saints, he began to weep much, and said: I have not lived a long
p. 12 time here. (f. 44 a) But it is about twenty years to-day since I came here.
But there are others who have dwelt here for forty years, and for fifty,
and for sixty, and for (f. 45 b) seventy years, who have dwelt in the same
place. For the place is level and plain, forty miles long, (f. 44 a) about
twelve miles broad; on its eastern side are rugged mountains, like a wall
inaccessible to those who do not know the place. A path crosses there.
(f. 45 b) On the west is the Red Sea, which extends, as people say, to
p. 13 the Ocean Sea. On its shore is a mountain (f. 44 b) from which issue twelve
springs of water; these and others beside them which trickle; and many other
wells among them. They issue (f. 45 a) from the mountain, and water many
palm-trees. And on that mountain are a number of anchorites dwelling,
and there is a church[1] (f. 44 b) below the mountain; and near the mountain
there were people truly heavenly who dwelt on the earth while their souls
were in heaven. About their discipline (f. 45 a) I am unable to speak, for not
one of them was led to us; nor about the conflict which took place, nor about
p. 14 their temptations from the devil (f. 73 b) which arose against them; I am not
able to tell, my beloved ones. Nevertheless I will speak about one or two
things. And it will be sufficient for the satisfaction of many, that those
who [hear me should know, from what I say, that the other things also are
of the same nature. A certain Moses] (f. 73 b) having adopted the discipline
of monasticism from his youth, practised monasticism for seventy-three years in
that mountain from which springs of water issued. [He dwelt in a certain cave
not far from the place [called] "Assemblies in Churches," truly another Elias,]
p. 15 (f. 73 a) for every time that he asked of God, it was done unto him. For God
did many mighty deeds by means of him. For He gave him power over wicked
spirits[1] [and by completely curing many he attached to the Christ nearly all the
people] (f. 73 a) in that desert, and also the people of the place the inhabitants
of Pharan, and made them Christians, for they were heathens, but now they are
p. 16 elect Christians. [For seeing signs and wonders which] (f. 4 a) the man of God,
Father Moses did, they believed in the Father, and in the Son, and in the Holy
Spirit. And they were persuaded to receive holy (f. 5 b) baptism. And as we
have said before about the servant of God, Father Moses, that he cured many
from their sicknesses, (f. 4 a) and from evil spirits, by the grace of our Lord

[1] Half a leaf of the MS is missing. Passages placed in brackets are not extant in Syriac.

Jesus the Christ. And this saint, from (the time that) he took the habit of the
Christ, ate no (f. 5 b) flesh[1], but he ate dates only. The people, the Saracens,
who dwelt there were bringing wheat from (f. 4 b) Egypt, which they p. 17
sometimes sold, and gave to us. And we gave them dates instead of the
wheat; from what we were gathering from the place. (f. 5 a) And we were
doing it [for] our necessity. The food of that saint was a few dates, and
water only. And he never tasted wine. (f. 4 b) And his dress was of palm-fibre
compressed. And he loved silence more than all men. And he received with
joy those who (f. 5 a) came to him to inquire from him about their thoughts. And
his sleep was after the liturgy of the night; and the rest (f. 13 a) of the hours he p. 18
spent in vigils. But in the days of fasting of the Forty he did not open the door
of the cave, until the fifth day of the (f. 10 b) Holy Week. On the days of the
fasting he said to us that we should serve him with these twenty dates, which
were beside him, and a pitcher of water (f. 13 a) only. And in one of those days
of fasting they brought unto him a man who was tried with an evil spirit.
This man was chief of Pharan. And when they arrived (f. 10 b) at the mountain
in which was the cave of the saint, the evil spirit tormented him, and he wailed
with a loud voice and said: "O Power! (f. 13 b) thou canst not thus even p. 19
for one hour make this aged man useless for his service." And forthwith the
demon came out of him and he was healed. He had been a heathen (f. 10 a) until
now, who had not received holy baptism. For all the Pharanites were heathen
formerly. And he returned to his house, (f. 13 b) whole; and he praised God,
he and those who were with him. But the servant of God did not open the
door of his cell, and he was not seen (f. 10 a) by any one of them.

What Father Psoes said about Father Moses is finished. (f. 42 a) *On account* p. 20
of Father Psoes the Egyptian.

And this Father Psoes dwelt there with Saba above Father Moses. And he
dwelt there forty (f. 47 b) years and he did not change from being with him.
And this one was taught by Psoes in the rule of a father, like his sign and seal.
(f. 42 a) And he took all that he heard and learnt from Saba. And I also
dwelt with him a little while from the beginning, and because of the hardness of
his regimen, I was forced (f. 47 b) to go out from beside him, for I could not bear
the regimen of hardness and torment of the body beside him. He also (f. 42 b)
was slain with the other holy fathers. We then make a remembrance of each p. 21
of the other holy fathers. I leave greater things than these that I may tell
(f. 47 a) what they did, and how they made known the rule of their struggle.
I recollect about one of them. The conduct of Father Joseph (f. 42 b) who
was from Elath, and he dwelt below the town two miles away from the
water. And he built himself a cell with his hands; and he (f. 47 a) was

[1] ܠܚܡܐ seems to be used in its Arabic meaning.

perfect by the grace of God. And he dwelt in that cell for thirty years;
and there was much discrimination in him, and he was full of the word
p. 22 (f. 53 a) of truth.

And he had one disciple. But he did not live with him, but near to
him. Now there came one of the brethren, that he might ask him about (f. 52 b)
his meditation, and he knocked on the door. But Saba was occupied with a vision
about God. And our brother stooped (f. 53 a) to the door and saw Saba, who
had become flames of fire from his head as far as to his feet. And our brother
said: "Trembling hath seized me, (f. 52 b) and I have become like a dead man."
And I fell down on the ground for an hour. And then I rose up, and sat near
p. 23 to the door. But Saba (f. 53 b) was occupied with a vision, and did not perceive
me. And after five hours he opened the door and brought me in. And when
we had prayed, we sat down. And Saba answered and said unto me, (f. 52 a)
"When didst thou come here?" And our brother said unto him, "I have
had four hours and more since I came hither, but (f. 53 b) that I might not
incommode thy Holiness, I did not knock." And Saba knew that our brother
had seen the vision. And he said nothing to him on account of this, but
all that he asked (f. 52 a) of him he told him. And he cured his thoughts;
and made him return in peace. And after that Saba also went away from that
p. 24 place and (f. 26 a) was seen no more by any one because of the glory of men.
But his disciple came whose name was Gelasius, and he did not find Saba,
and he sought him, and did not find (f. 31 b) him. And then he dwelt in Saba's
cell, and was much grieved because of him.

Beginning of a chapter. But after (f. 26a) six years, in the middle of the day,
a man knocked at the door, and our brother went out and beheld Saba his own
Abbot standing; and amazement took hold of him, and he (f. 31 b) thought that
he was a spirit. And he said unto him with composure, "Pray, Father." And
when he had prayed, he received him with joy; and they asked about each (f. 26 b)
p. 25 other. And Saba said unto him: "Thou hast done well, my son, that first thou
hast sought for a prayer, for many are the snares of the Enemy." And his (f. 31 a)
disciple said unto him: "What happened to thee, Father, that thou didst depart
from thy flock, and didst leave me an orphan? And I have grieved much."

And Saba said unto him: "The reason why (f. 26 b) I have not been seen
by thee, God is He who knoweth it. But yet until this hour I have not been
far from this place; and I have spent no First day of the week that I have not
(f. 31 a) taken part with you in the Holy Mysteries of the Christ."

And our brother wondered at his meditations; and how he came in and went
p. 26 out (f. 14 a) amongst them; and no one saw him. And our brother said unto
him: "What is the reason that thou hast come to thy servant to-day?" And
Saba said unto him: (f. 9 b) "To-day I am going to the Lord; and I came to thee

that thou mightest bury my body. And, bury it as thou wilt." (f. 14 a) And
Saba spoke much to our brother about the destiny of his soul. And in that hour
Saba stretched out his hands to heaven, and prayed, and slept in peace. And
our brother, (f. 9 b) his disciple, ran immediately and assembled the holy fathers.
And we took branches of palm-trees and we went and with songs (f. 14 b)
and with psalms we brought him into the church. And his face was p. 27
shining like a light. And we kept a vigil over him all the night. And we
laid (f. 9 a) him with the saints who slept there in the place. And these holy
fathers were perfect and excellent in their discipline, (f. 14 b) and in prayer,
and in their own polity. And we were forty-three dwelling in that place.

And behold, two men came from across the sea; (f. 9 a) and they told us
that they had crossed the sea on boats of palm-wood. And they told us to take
care of ourselves, for behold! many Blemmyes had come (f. 65 a) suddenly and p. 28
seized a boat which was beyond Elath, and said unto us, "Conduct us to Clysma,
and we will not kill you." And we said unto them, (f. 70 b) in our fear lest they
should kill us: "We thank you, and we are waiting till the south wind blows,
(f. 65 a) and we shall set sail as you wish. But we found by the power of God,
by night, how we might escape out of their hands. And behold, we tell you:
(f. 70 b) Give heed and keep watch that they do not come here sometime,
and slay all of you."

And when we heard these things we were (f. 65 b) in great fear; and we p. 29
placed spies on the shore of the sea; (saying) If ye see a ship coming, ye
shall inform us. And after a day a little ship was seen (f. 70 a) towards the
evening coming towards us. And the Saracens and the Pharanites also who were
to be found there came up and prepared to make war with the (f. 65 b) Blemmyes, for the sake of their women and their children. And they were assembled
to the number of two hundred men, beside the women and their children upon
the mountain which is above (f. 70 a) the palm-trees, where there are fountains
of water. But we fled to our church, which is fortified with bricks, and the height
of its wall is three statures of a man (f. 29 a) and when these Barbarians arrived p. 30
at the shore of the sea, and by means of the sailors who brought them they
remained there, on the shore (f. 28 b) of the sea all that night. But when it
dawned, and became morning they chained the sailors of the ship, that they
might not run away, (f. 29 a) with the ship. And they left one of the sailors still
standing upon the ship, with one of them[selves], lest they should take the ship.

And they crossed the mountain, and came as far as the springs (f. 28 b) of water.
And the Saracens of that place met them for a fight, between the hill and the
springs of water. And archers of both (f. 29 b) were shooting arrows. But p. 31
the Barbarians were numerous and skilled in war, and they chased the

Saracens, and killed a hundred and forty-seven (f. 28 b) of them. And the rest fled to the (shelter ?) of the mountains, and some of them were hid amongst the trees. And the Barbarians sat down after (f. 29 b) the fight had ceased. They took their women and children captive, and all that belonged to them. And they gave (i.e. distributed) them where the springs of water are. And after these things they ran fast (f. 28 a) like wild beasts and came upon us to the fortress where we had fled; and they were expecting that they would find [much hidden treasure. As they were walking round the walls screaming, and filling the air with wild howls, and threats in barbarous languages, we all spent the time in much sadness of spirit, quite destitute of counsel, with our eyes fixed on God, prostrate in mind, overflowing in prayer. And some of our people bore the ills with a strenuous, equal mind, others lamented; one gave thanks, pouring himself out in prayers; another consoled his neighbours, and all together exclaimed, "Lord! have mercy!"

But our most holy Father, who was named Paul, a native of Petra, said in the midst of the assembly: "Hearken, ye fathers and brethren, unto me a sinner, and the least of all. Ye all know, that we have dwelt in this place for the sake of our Lord and Master, Jesus the Christ, cut off, because of His love, from the habits of this vain world, in this rough and fearful desert, we the unworthy and sinful, who will bear His yoke, living in hunger, in thirst, in dire poverty and misery despising certainly, if I may so say, everything earthly and this vain world, that we may deserve to be His worthy companions in the kingdom of heaven. And now nothing will happen, or will come near to us even in this hour, except by His command and will. Therefore if He wishes to free us from this vain and changeful life, and take us to Himself, it is right that we should rejoice in His name, and exult, and give thanks and in no wise be sad. For what could be more joyful, what more sweet, than to look on His glory, and His awful countenance? Recall to memory, fathers and brethren, how always, when seated together, we have preached (about) the blessed saints to each other, who for His holy Name, have endured martyrdom and have wished that we also might be found their companions in the City. Lo therefore, my children, the time is come,
p. 32 and] (f. 36 a) it is given unto you to inherit life eternal with them, as is your desire, that you should be with them in this gladness which is prepared for all these (f. 37 b) who please the Lord Jesus. Because of this, be not afflicted, O athletes of the Christ! by this good conflict; and let it not grieve (f. 36 a) you, and let not your souls be faint[1], and do nothing that is unworthy of our cowl. But be clothed with strength and joy and manliness (f. 37 b), that ye may endure with pure and brave heart; and may God receive you into His kingdom."

[1] Literally "let not your souls be made little."

And they all answered and said: "Yea, our honoured Father (f. 36 b), as thou hast said unto us, thus will we do. What shall we render unto the Lord for all that He hath given unto us? We will take the cup of salvation, and call upon the holy name of (f. 37 a) the Lord." Ps. 116. 12 p. 33

And then our Father lifted up his hands to heaven and said, "Lord Jesus the Christ, Son of the living God, (f. 36 b) Who never dieth, forget not Thy servants, but remember our afflictions, and our poverty; and strengthen us in this hour of affliction, and receive our offering of a sacrifice, as a sweet savour before Thee. For to Thee belongeth honour and glory for ever. [Amen."

Then, while we were saying, Amen, a voice came as if from the altar, heard by us all, "Come unto Me, all ye who labour, and are heavy laden, and I will restore you." At that voice, all were seized with terror; the hearts and the knees of all were loosened, which made it plain that the spirit was willing, as the Lord said, but the flesh was weak. But the faces of all were fixed only on heaven; we were all now lacking in hope of this life. Then the Barbarians, as no one opposed or retarded their onrush, climbed up over a heap of tree trunks, piled up like a wall, and the door being opened, ran in like ravening wolves, huge, rough animals, with their swords firmly grasped in their hands. But first they seized a certain man named Jeremiah sitting at the door of the Lord's church and commanded him, by means of one of their own number who fulfilled the duty of interpreting, to shew which was our President. He being fearless at these things, not in the least terrified, either at the rough look of the Barbarians, or at the sharp points of the drawn (swords), said: "I neither fear you, O impious ones and enemies of God, nor will I shew you him whom ye seek, although I have him standing near me."

The Barbarians were astounded at the great boldness of the man, and the firm strength of his heart, that he did not fear them in the very least, but accused them with a reproof; and having seized him everywhere, they bound him hand and foot, and set him up as a target, and loaded him with such a rain of arrows, that they left no place in his body free from arrows. Thus wrestling bravely against the devil, he obtained the crown first of all, the serpent's head being trampled to death; the holy firstfruits, having become a fine example to the saints. When our most holy Father Paul saw these things, he came forward immediately shouting and saying: "I am he whom ye seek!" and he shewed himself to them with his own finger, that he was he whom they sought. He declared himself thus, fearing nothing, to be a brave servant of the Christ, he counted in his soul neither the blows nor the torture which the wicked men were going to bring in before the massacre. Having therefore seized him, they asked, where was his money hidden. To whom he said with soft speech, and gentleness of manners, as was his wont, "Believe me, children, in all my substance, except these old haircloths, with which, as you see, I am clothed, I possess nothing." With these words, he stretched out his cloak with his hand and shewed it to them.

But they, beating his bare neck with stones, and piercing his cheeks and his face with arrows, "Bring," they said, "what thou possessest." But after the torture had been prolonged for a long hour, and they had mocked him, and had found nothing, then they drove a sword through the middle of his skull, cutting his sacred head into two halves, and dropping them down over either shoulder; and verily all his body having received other blows, and many torments having been endured by his force of mind before his death, he lay at the feet of the Father who was already dead. Plainly he was another victor, a brilliant triumpher over the devil, being cowardly in not a single thing, or having become weaker in spirit.

But I, the miserable one, having seen this great slaughter, and the streams of the saints' blood, and their viscera thrown about, was frozen by fear, looked about, considering silently, in what place I could find safety As there was in the corner of the house, in the left hand, a heap made of a few palm-branches and the Barbarians being in the meantime busied with torturing Paul], (f. 74 a)
p. 34 I fled, and hid myself there. And I thought that one of two things would
happen to me. Either I would escape, or I would be taken, (f. 81 b) and they would kill me. But these wicked Barbarians left two fathers, whom they had slain in the court, and rushed suddenly into the church, (f. 74 a) shouting together with drawn swords in their hands, and every one whom they met there, they slew without mercy. For some of them (f. 81 b) they smote on their heads, and another on his shoulder. But what can I say [for just as each had received a blow, they slew him].

p. 35 (f. 74 b) While he was relating these things to us, he wept, and his tears fell
like floods of water, so that we all wept also. And again (f. 81 a) he said unto us: "What shall I say? how shall I relate what mine eyes have seen? [There was one there named Salathiel, who had as kinsman a monk in the Institute. He was] (f. 74 b) about fifteen years old. Father Joseph had taught him from his childhood the discipline of monasticism. For from his childhood he sent him out to the desert to fight (f. 81 a) against Satan; and in hunger and thirst.
p. 36 When the Barbarians saw this one also, that he was a boy, the wicked men
(f. 20 a) did not wish to kill him; but yet one of them took him out.

Beginning of a chapter. And when our brother saw that he was not (f. 17 a) worthy to be slain with these saints by wicked men, [he seized a sword from the Barbarians, from the one who] held (f. 20 a) him. And he struck

one of them on the shoulder that it might happen (that) they should kill him.
For this was his longing to die with these (f. 17b) saints, that he might be slain
by these hateful men. Then they raged against him with anger, and flung
(themselves) at him, and gnashed (f. 20b) their teeth upon him, and cut p. 37
him limb by limb. And he rejoiced and said: "Blessed be the Lord, Who
hath not delivered me into the hands of the wicked." And whilst he (f. 17a)
said these things, he finished his course in the Lord. And after he was
dead they struck him often; and when I saw these things I entreated God
(f. 20b) to cover me from their eyes, that they might not see me; so that
I might escape and bury the bodies of the saints who had been slain there.
And they filled all the (f. 17a) church with blood, the blood of the saints
who had been slain. And it was finished according to every good wish,
and they praised God for these (f. 1a) things that had happened to them. p. 38
For their thoughts were in heaven with the Lord their God; and they were holy
temples to God most High. (f. 8 b) And they left the transient and perishing
world, and cleaved only unto God. And thus they died by the sword. (f. 1 a)
And they were not separated from the love of the Christ; as it is written,
"Who shall separate us from the love of the Christ? neither sword, nor Rom. 8.
tribulation shall separate us (f. 8 b) from the love of the Christ." Thus these 35
holy ones resigned their bodies to tribulation and to the sword If then
(f. 1 b) I call them martyrs, I am not wrong; for they endured tribulation. p. 39
They were completely cut to pieces, limb by limb, like martyrs. (f. 8a) But
the Barbarians were thinking that they had killed them all; and they were
searching in all places, hoping that they would find (f. 1 b) gold. And they
did not know that the saints possessed nothing upon the earth. But when
I had seen all these things done, I (nearly) died from fear. And not a drop
of blood still remained in me; but I remained like a dead man. I was hidden
among the palm-branches, for I had said: (22 a) "For here they will seek and will p. 40
find me." (f. 22 a) And I was thrown among the palm-branches; while they
came towards me, and I saw my death (f. 15 b) with my eyes. And I begged
of God that if it were His will, I might escape from them. And they came
as far as (my) corner. And when they (f. 22 a) saw these palm-branches,
they despised them, and went off from me; for God covered their (eyes)
that they did not see me. And they left the saints (f. 15 b) thrown one
upon the other. And when they found nothing to take, they returned to
the side of the springs (f. 22 b) of water. And they tried to sail on the p. 41
sea; and go to Clysma, where it had been their desire before to go. And
they went, (f. 15 a) and found the ship broken, and their comrade killed,
him whom they had left to take care of the ship. He was a friend of the

Christ; (f. 22 b) and he could have fled secretly away from the Barbarians who were with him in the ship. And he cut the ropes of the ship, and she knocked suddenly against a rock and she was broken.

And he killed the Barbarian who was with him in the ship, and threw
his body into the sea. And by the mercy of God he escaped to the
p. 42 mountain. (f. 59 a) And they then saw a broken ship, and their comrade
killed, and the confidence of their hope was cut off. And they were considering as to how they should return (f. 62 a) to their place. And they
could not *do it*, because their ship was broken. And in a rage they killed
the women and the children. And afterwards they kindled a fire (f. 59 a) in
the palm-trees. And they burnt many of the palm-trees ruthlessly; so that
they might lay waste the place. And while they were doing these things,
men came from Pharan, (f. 62) valiant chosen men, six hundred in number,
and the Barbarians were mourning because of their country. And when they
p. 43 had agreed (together), (f. 59 b) and had heard of the massacre, they came like
wild beasts. Then the Barbarians also prepared themselves for the fight,
and withdrew (f. 62 b) themselves a little from the water. And they began
the battle from the rising of the sun in a level place. And they hurled
arrows the one upon the other. (f. 59 b) But the Pharanites were more
numerous than the Barbarians, and they slew the Barbarians. But the
Barbarians gave up[1] the hope of their lives, (f. 62 a) for they were not able
to run away, that they might escape. Then they rose up in strength, and
p. 44 endured much in the fight. And the fight was (f. 46 a) until the ninth hour.
And they killed in that day of the Pharanites eighty-four men, and many who
were wounded in the battle here did not die. (f. 43 b) The Blemmyes stood
well in the fight because of their children until they were all slain; and not
one was left of them. (f. 46 a) But I, [while these things were happening],
recovered strength and came out from my corner where I was hidden. And
I sought to bury (f. 43 b) the bodies of the saints. And I found them all
who had been killed except three, Domnus, and Orion, and Andrew. And
p. 45 Domnus was in great torment, (f. 46 b) for he was badly wounded in the
side, but not unto death. And Orion was not with him. And he suffered
nothing at all, for the Barbarian (f. 43 a) who struck him with the sword in his
abdomen from right to left thought that he had killed him, but did not hurt
him at all. (f. 46 b) He only cut his garment, and did not touch his body.
And he was thrown among the bodies of the saints as dead. And he saw
me, and he arose (f. 43 a) and went round the bodies of the saints with
me. And he was afflicted and grieved at all that had happened to the

[1] Literally "cut off."

saints. But the Pharanites (f. 66 a) after they had gone to the Blemmyes p. 46
had left their bodies on the shore of the sea to the beasts of the earth,
and to the fowls of the heaven. But those of them[selves] who had been
killed, (f. 71 a) they collected, and made a great wailing over them. And
they buried them at the foot of the mountain, above (f. 66 a) the springs
of water in a cave. And they came to us, and they saw us weeping and
wailing about the saints who were slain. And they entered and saw the
bodies of the saints, (f. 71 a) torn, and they wailed and wept bitterly, seeing
the flock of the Christ torn and flung (f. 66 b) upon the earth. But we were p. 47
in great fear, seeing the blows that had struck the bodies of the saints, the slaves
of the Christ, those who in their lives (f. 71 a) had pleased the Christ, and in
their deaths gave the blood of their necks that they might be finished with
the holy martyrs.

(f. 66 b) *Beginning of a chapter.* But Obedianus, the chief of Pharan, with
the great men of Pharan, brought very costly garments, and covered the
bodies of the saints, for they also had heard the word (f. 71 a), "I was Matt. 25. 36
naked, and they clothed me." But Domnus was from Rome, and the saints
were (f. 48 a) thirty-nine. And Domnus who was from Rome, his life p. 48
was still in him. And all those who were there took (f. 41 b) branches of
palm-trees, and came to meet the saints. And with praise and with honour
we buried them all (f. 48 a) in a certain place near to the camp. And
Domnus died in the evening. And we buried him, not with the saints,
but near them. The reason was (f. 41 b) that we should not open the grave
and disturb the bodies of the saints. But he was counted with them; forty
Martyrs (f. 48 b) of the Lord Jesus the Christ. To Whom be glory for ever p. 49
and ever, Amen.

And Father Andrew and Father Orion remained there (f. 41 a) in the place;
hesitating in their minds whether they should go or stay. But I, because
I was not able to endure the hardships of the desolations (f. 48 b) of that place,
nor to cease from the grief for the fathers who were slain there, I thought of
going to Your Holinesses. And Obedianus was a great lover (f. 41 a) of the
Christ. He persuaded me to stay in the place, and he said unto me: "I will
care for thee, and I will supply thy wants at every (f. 35 a) season." And I did p. 50
not stay, because of the desolation of the place, but I have said to you truly
what happened there. (f. 38 b) Do you also tell me what has happened
in your neighbourhood truly concerning those who have been slain there.

And we told him all truly (f. 35 a) about what has happened amongst
us in detail. And we marvelled at the wonderful things of God, that
thus on the same day all the saints (f. 38 b) both here and there were

equally crowned, and again that they were the same in number; and we
p. 51 exceeded with weeping about what was said. (f. 35 b) And after this the
Governor of the place rose up, Father Doulos, and said: "O my beloved
ones! these saints also, so worthy of the Christ and chosen by Him, became
(f. 38 a) servants of God, and worthy of the kingdom of heaven; and after
their conflict and battling and temptations (f. 35 b) obtained the crown of
their martyrdom with God. For behold they dwell in ineffable glory. But
let us arise and care about ourselves. And that we may persuade them to
seek from our Lord Jesus on our behalf that He may make us also worthy of
p. 52 the kingdom, (f. 61 a) and the glory of their deeds: Amen. And let us
glorify God, and thank Him from all our soul that according to His mercy
He hath saved us (f. 60 a) from the hands of the Barbarians. [And let us
seek with vows, that we may be slain with the holy Martyrs." Having spoken
these things, he consoled all with words composed for the profit of souls.]

(f. 61 a) But I, Ammonius, returned to Egypt, and truly I [took] with me all
these writings on parchment. And I went to Egypt, (f. 60 a) but not to my
first place, whose name was Canopus, but near to Memphis, [and shut myself
p. 53 into a very small hut] (f. 61 b) and I read every hour in the memoirs of the
holy Martyrs of the Christ, that I might delight in the memory of their
struggles. And at every time I praised (f. 60 a) God the Father, the Ruler
of all, to Whom be glory for ever and ever, Amen.

I John found writings, (f. 61 b) by the mercy of our Lord Jesus the Christ, beside the monk Tarus near Naukratis, in the Egyptian tongue; and I translated them by the grace of the Christ into the Greek tongue, for I was cognizant of both tongues, Egyptian and Greek. And by the grace of (f. 34 a) God I translated them accurately, to the praise of the holy witnesses, And may the Lord Jesus give us a portion with them all in His Kingdom. Amen.

The life of the Holy Fathers who were slain at Mount Sinai and Raïtho, is finished, in the days of Pope Peter of Alexandria. But the memory of these holy ones is made in December in the months of the Romans, the 28th. May the Lord have mercy on us by their prayers, and on all the world.

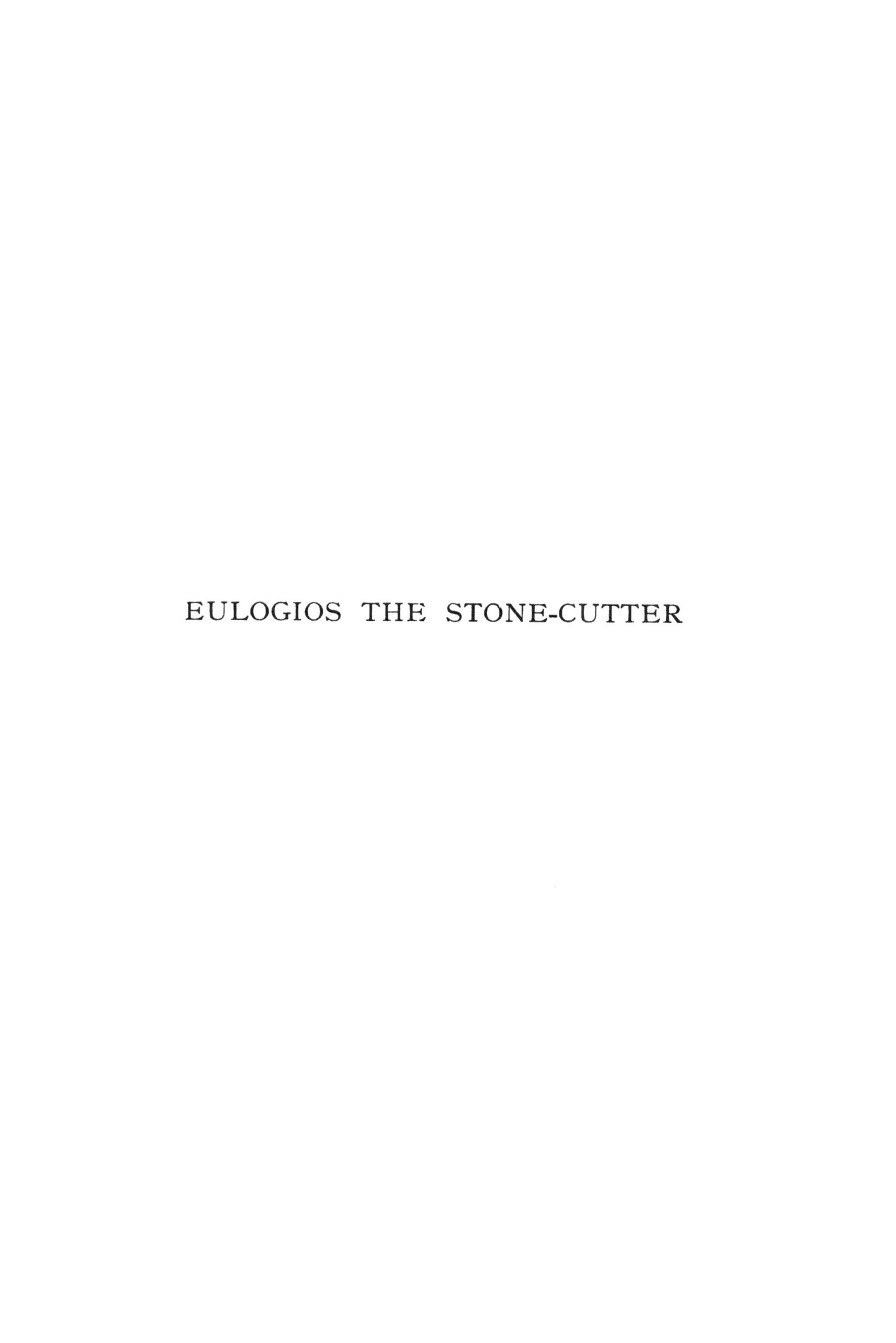

EULOGIOS THE STONE-CUTTER

PART II

THE LIFE OF EULOGIOS THE EGYPTIAN, WHO WAS A STONE-CUTTER

FATHER Daniel, the priest of Scete, said: Once upon a time I went to
Thebais, with one of my disciples, and we sat (f. 34 b) in a ship, and we p. 55
came down to the river. And when we arrived at a village, the old man persuaded those who were in the ship, for he said: "It is necessary that we should remain here to-day." And they alighted there. And his disciple began to murmur and said: "How long shall we go round about? Let us go to Scete?" (f. 34 b) And the old man said: "Nay, but we will stay here to-day." And they sat down in the midst of the village as is the custom of strangers. And our brother said to the old man: "Is it pleasing (f. 39 a) to God that we should sit like beggars? Let us go for a testimony." And the old man said: "Nay, but we will sit here."

For the old man (f. 67 b) knew by the Spirit that Eulogios was coming from p. 56
Africa to his former places. And because of this the old man waited for him, that other one, but he did not (f. 70 a) know which was the place. And they waited sitting there until the evening. And they did not eat, and they did not drink. And one brother began (f. 67 b) to contend with the old man, and he said: "Oh! because thou art a servant of the Christ, because of thee I have to die."

And while they were talking a certain old man of the city came, tall of stature, (f. 70 a) and full of years; and his head was white, and he was bent with age. And when he saw Father Daniel, he ran and embraced him and
began to kiss him. (f. 67 a) And he wept and greeted his disciple. And he p. 57
said unto them: "If ye are naming the Lord, come with me to my house." And he carried a lantern, in which was a lamp, and went round about (f. 70 b) in that street of the town and sought for strangers. And he led the old man and his disciple and every stranger whom he found and brought them to his house (f. 76 a) and washed the feet of the brethren and of the old man. But there was no man in his house, nor even in another place, save God only. And he

set (f. 70 b) a table before them. And when they were satisfied, he took the
crumbs, and gave them to the dogs of the village. For thus he did, (f. 2 a) and
p. 58 left nothing till the morning. And he brought the old man alone, and they sat
talking the one with the other to the profit of the soul, (f. 7 b) with many tears,
until the morning. And in the morning they saluted each other, and went on
the way. And as they were going on the way, our brother made a repentance (f. 2 a) for his Abbot, and said: "Do me a favour, father, and tell me
who is that old man, and whence dost thou know him? And the old man
did not wish to tell him. Again (f. 7 b) our brother made a repentance and
entreated him, saying: "Thou hast revealed much good to me, father, and
concerning this (matter) thou hast not revealed to me, father." For he said
p. 59 unto (f. 2 b) our brother much about the virtues of the saints; but the old
man did not wish to reveal to our brother about that (other) old man.

And then our brother was vexed and did not speak with the old man until
he came (f. 7 a) to Scete. And when our brother went to his cell, he did not
take anything to eat to the old man, as was his wont, for at eleven o'clock
(f. 2 b) he ate every day of his life. But when it was evening, the old man
came to our brother and said: "Why, my son, hast thou left thy father
now to die of hunger?" And he said: "I have (f. 7 a) no father, for if
I had a father, he would love his son."

And the old man said unto him: "Then be in peace!" And the old
p. 60 man held the door to open (it), and go away. And our brother ran and held
him, and began to kiss him and say: "As God liveth, I will not leave thee,
until thou tell (f. 75 b) me who that old man was. For our brother could not
see the old man hurt, for he loved him much. And then he said unto him:
"Make me (f. 80 b) some food, and afterwards I will tell thee."

And while the old man was eating, he said unto our brother, "Be not
stiff-necked, for because thou didst quarrel with me, I did not tell thee when
we were (f. 75 b) sitting in the village, and I did not reveal (it) to thee. Thou
also do not repeat to any man what I say unto thee."

And he said this unto him: (f. 80 b) 'This old man is called Eulogios. And
p. 61 his craft is (that of) a stone-mason. And he uses one carob every day, and
fasts till the evening, tasting nothing. And in the evening (f. 75 a) he comes
to the village and every stranger whom he finds, he brings him to his house,
and feeds them. And what is over he gives to the dogs, (f. 80 b) until
to-day. And to-day he is a hundred and twenty years old. And he uses one
carob every day.

When I was young, forty years ago, (f. 75 a) I went up to sell the work of
my hands in this town, in which we are. And in the evening he came and led

me and the brethren who were with me, as was his wont, and refreshed (f. 68 a)
us, being strangers[1]. But when I came to my cell, and I knew the discipline of p. 62
the excellent man I fasted two weeks (f. 69 b) and I persuaded God to give
him a blessing, that thus he might refresh the brethren as he pleased. And
when I had fasted three weeks, I lay (f. 68 a) like a dead man for much more
than a day.

And I saw a man coming towards me in an honourable form. And he said
unto me: "What is wrong with thee, Daniel?" And I said: (f. 69 a) "My
Lord, I have given a word to the Christ, that I will not eat bread until He
hears me concerning Eulogios, the stone-mason, that thus He would give
(f. 68 b) him (wherewith) he may also help others." And he said unto me: p. 63
"It is well." And I said unto Him: "I pray Thee, my Lord, give him, so
that all men may glorify Thy holy name because of him."

And He said unto me: "I have said unto thee that it is well. But if thou
desirest that I should give him, give a pledge to Me (f. 68 b) for his soul that
it may be saved with much possessions." And I gave (it) to Him. Then I said
unto Him: "At my hands seek his soul." And I saw (f. 69 a) as if we were
standing in (the church of) our Lady of the Holy Resurrection, and behold, a boy
was sitting on the holy stone. And Eulogios (f. 24 a) *was* standing on his right p. 64
hand. And this boy sent to me one of those who were standing before him.
And he brought me to his side. And he said unto me: "Art thou he who gave
a pledge for Eulogios?" (f. 23 b) And all those who were standing answered
and said, "Yea, our Lord." And then he said: "Tell him, Thy pledge will be
required." And I said: "Yea, my Lord, thou shalt (f. 24 a) seek it at my hands;
but add a blessing to it." And I saw two of them who were turning much
wealth into the bosom of Eulogios. (f. 23 b) And all that they were turning
he received in his bosom. And I awoke, and glorified God.

Beginning of a chapter. And Eulogios went out (f. 24 b) to his work as was p. 65
his custom; and behold, while he knocked on the stone, (he) heard like the noise
of something, and found a small hole. And again (f. 23 a) he knocked and found
a cave full of gold. And then he wondered and said: "This gold belonged to the
children of Israel. What then shall I do? If I take (f. 24 b) it to the village,
the prince will hear of it, and take it; and I also will fall into great danger.
But I shall take it to another place where (f. 23 a) no man knoweth me." And
then he hired camels as if to carry stones. And in the night he carried the gold,
and conveyed it to the shore of the river.

(f. 11 a) And he left off the good work that he had done. And he took a p. 66

[1] Literally "our strangerhood."

ship and sailed to Constantinople. And at this time the Emperor Justinus
(f. 12 b) was reigning, the son of Justinian. And Eulogios offered much gold
to the Emperor and to all the magnates of the Emperor; that he might
become (f. 11 a) Eparch over all the Eparchy. And he bought a great property
which is called Egyptian until this day. And it happened (f. 12 b) that after
two years I saw again this boy in my dream in the holy church; and I said
p. 67 to myself: "Where then (f. 11 b) is Eulogios?" And after a little I saw an
Ethiopian drawing Eulogios. And he brought him out in the presence of
the Prefecture. And when I awoke, (f. 12 a) I said: "Woe is me, the sinner,
the miserable one, for I have destroyed my soul." And while I was thus in
thought I arose (f. 11 b) and I took my basket for a wallet. And I said to
that boy: "I seek for Eulogios." And I sat down there like a man who is selling
the work of his hands (f. 12 a) and I waited for Eulogios as was my custom,
and *that of* all the brethren. But when it was evening, and become very dark
p. 68 (f. 32 a) and no man received me, I arose and found an old woman, and said
unto her trustfully: "Mother, give me three cakes that I may eat. I am hungry
(f. 25 b) for I have eaten nothing to-day."

And she said unto me: "I will give thee." And she went and brought me
cooked food and bread, and she sat down beside me (f. 32 a) and began to speak
to me words of cheer. And she said unto me: "Dost thou not know that thou
art a boy? and it is not good for thee to come to the village? Dost thou not
(f. 25 b) know that a monk seeketh quiet?" And other good words she said
unto me. And I said again unto her: "And what dost thou think we should
p. 69 do? (f. 32 b) I came to sell the work of my hands."

And she said unto me: "Even if thou dost sell thy work, do not linger in
the village; but if thou seekest to be (f. 25 a) a monk, go to Scete."

Beginning of a chapter. But I said unto her: "Thy breakfast is quite safe
from these mockeries; is there (f. 32 b) not one man who fears God in this
village, who will receive strangers?"

And she said unto me: "O my lord! what hast thou said? We had a man,
a hewer of (f. 25 a) stones. And he did a great deal of good to strangers. And
p. 70 God saw his good deeds, and gave him much wealth, and he (f. 51 a) it is
who is Eparch to-day." And when I heard that he had been made Eparch,
I said to myself, that it was I who had done this murder; (f. 54 b) and I had
thrown this man into the ship and then I had gone up to Constantinople. And
I inquired where was the house of the Egyptian. And they told me. And I
sat (f. 51 a) at the doors of his house, until he came out. And I saw him coming
out with a great train. And I called, and I said: "Have mercy upon me, and
hear (f. 54 b) from me what I seek to say unto thee." And he did not even

look; but those also who were going before him struck me. And again I spoke (f. 51 b) to them in this way every other time, and they struck me. p. 71

And I spent four weeks, and never could come near him. Then when I went out I threw myself before (f. 54 a) an ikon of the Lady Mary with weeping. And I said: "Lord Jesus the Christ (Son of God), have mercy (f. 51 b) upon me and release me from the pledge of that man. And if not, then I will go to the world." And while these things [happened] that I saw and knew (f. 54 a) with my eyes, I approached the crowd, and I heard there the voice of a great mob, saying: "Behold, the Queen of the world." And there went before her (f. 21 a) thousands and myriads of people. And I called and p. 72
said: "O my Lady, have mercy on me." And she said unto me: "What hast thou?" And I told her that I had given a pledge for (f. 16 b) Eulogios the Eparch. "But command that I may be loosed from my pledge for him." And she said: "I am not able to do as thou dost ask, fulfil thy pledge."

(f. 21 a) And I awoke, and then I said: "If I were to die I will not depart from his door until I have talked with him." And I went and sat down where the door of his house was. And when he passed, I approached and the door-keeper ran towards me; and gave me blows until my skin was chafed. Then my spirit was faint (f. 21 b) from the blows, and from what they were threatening p. 73
me with. And then I said: "I will go my way to Scete. And if I had sought God He would have delivered me, and also Eulogios" (f. 16 a). And then I went, and sought an Alexandrian ship, that I might go to my place. And I found a ship, and went up into it, so that I might come to my cell.

(f. 21 b) And when I had gone up to the ship, from faintness of soul I slept. And while I was sleeping, I saw as if I were in *the church of the* Holy Resurrection, (f. 16 a) and I saw the boy sitting on a stone before the Holy Sepulchre. And he looked at me with great anger; and for fear of him (f. 77 a) all my body trembled, and I was not able to open my mouth, and my heart was p. 74
dried up within me. And he said unto me: "Where is thy pledge?" And he told two (f. 78 b) of those who stood before him to chain me, and to hang me up with my hands bound behind me. And he said unto me: "Do not give a pledge for a man which is beyond thy power (f. 77 a) and thou art contradicting **Ben-Sira viii. 13**
God." And I was not able to open my mouth. And while I was hanging, a voice came saying: "Lo! the Queen has come out." And when I saw her, (f. 78 b) I took courage.

And I said unto her in an humble tone, "Have mercy on me, O Queen of the world!" And she said unto me: "What dost thou seek?" And I said unto her: (f. 77 b) "I am hanging because of the pledge of Eulogios." And she said p. 75
unto me: "I will intercede for thee." And I saw her go out; and she kissed

the feet of that boy. (f. 78 a) And immediately they let me down, as I was hanging. And the boy said unto me: "Henceforth never do this thing." I said: (f. 77 b) "Lo, my Lord, for because of this thou hast convinced me, so that I shall be more careful. I have sinned; forgive me."

And he commanded, and they released me. And he said unto me: (f. 78 b) "Go thy way to thy cell, and I will send Eulogios to his former work, and do not grieve."

p. 76 *Beginning of a chapter.* Then when I awoke (f. 40 a) I came into a
great rejoicing, for I was released from the pledge of Eulogios. And then I
sailed on the sea praising God. And after three months Justinus the king died,
(f. 33 b) and Justinianus reigned, and there rebelled against him Hephitios, and
Axicrates, and Pompinus, and Eulogios the Eparch. And those (f. 40 a) three
fought, and all their wealth was plundered; and also the property of Eulogios,
and all his wealth. And he fled by night (f. 33 b) alone, in the clothes that
were upon his body. And he went out of Constantinople. And the king
p. 77 commanded that wheresoever Eulogios the Egyptian should be found, (f. 40 b)
he should die the death. And he fled and came to his village, and changed his
clothes (to be) like those of the villagers. And all the village was assembled
about him, that they might see him. And they said: (f. 33 a) "We have heard
that thou hast become a Patrician." And he said unto them: "Yea, but if I had
become a Patrician, was it right that I should see you? Nay, but it was another
Eulogios from this place. For I was in Jerusalem praying." And then he came
to his [right] mind, and said (f. 33 a) to himself: "O poor Eulogios! arise, take
thine iron pick-axe, and go and work, where there is no palace, lest thy head
p. 78 be taken off."

(f. 57 a) And he took the iron pick-axe and went out to the wine-press where he had found the gold, expecting that he would find other gold there. And he knocked for six hours (f. 64 b) and found nothing. And he began to remember those viands, and that honour, and the delight of the deception that was in them, and he said: (f. 57 a) "Arise, work, Eulogios, for here it is Egypt." And thus little by little he came back to his own former habits, by the grace of our Lord Jesus. For (f. 64 b) God is not unjust, to forget his former works which he did.

p. 79 And after a little time I went up to that village. (f. 57 b) Now when he saw me in the evening, he came and conducted me as *was* his wont. But when I saw him I sighed and wept, and I said: (f. 64 a) "How great are Thy works, O Lord! Thou hast done everything in the world. Thou humblest, and Thou raisest up. Thy judgments and Thy wondrous works who can (f. 57 b) search out? O Lord God. But I have sinned in what I have offended. My soul hath almost dwelt in Sheol."

And he took water, and washed my feet, as was his wont, and he arranged a table. And after we had eaten, I said unto him: "What art thou doing, Father Eulogios?"

(f. 6 a) And he said unto me: "Pray for me, my lord, for I am poor, and there p. 80
is nothing in my hands." And I said unto him: "Eulogios, what was thine was not thine." And he said unto me: (f. 3 b) "Why, my lord Abbot, have I offended thee in anything?" And I said unto him: "In what hast thou not offended me?" And then I told him all, and also about the blows (f. 6 a) which I received from the door-keeper. And we wept together. And he said unto me: "Pray that God may send me a blessing. And henceforth I shall make myself worthy." And I said unto him: "Believe me, (f. 3 b) my lord Eulogios, that henceforth thou shalt not expect to be entrusted with anything of this world, but
with one carob every day (f. 6 b)." And behold! all this time God was arming him p. 81
and strengthening him. And every day he used one carob. Behold also I have told thee where I knew him.'

(f. 3 a) And the disciple of the old man wondered at all that he endured because of the pledge of Eulogios. These things Father Daniel revealed (f. 6 b) to his disciple after he returned from the Thebaid. It behoves us to wonder at the love of God, that thus in a short time He exalteth and humiliateth, just as in our own trading. Pray then that we also may be made humble by the fear of our Lord Jesus the Christ; that we may find
(f. 49 a) mercy before the awful judgment-seat, by the myriads of the prayers of p 82
all the saints. Amen.

WHAT FATHER DANIEL RELATED TO HIS DISCIPLE ABOUT PATRICIA

Father Daniel related about a certain eunuch who was in the desert in the interior of Scete. (f. 49 a) And his cell was distant about eighteen miles from Scete. And once upon a time he went beside Father Daniel, on the sabbath, at night, (f. 56 b) and no man knew of it except his disciple alone. And the old man commanded his disciple to fill for him one pitcher of water every (f. 49 b)
p. 83 week; and to place it near the door. And he knocked and went his way that he might not talk with him. But he (left) a potsherd near the mouth of the cave on which was written: "Bring it." (f. 56 a) And thus our brother did. He filled for him a pitcher of water every week. And the old man had written on the potsherd what he needed; and our brother (f. 49 b) placed the pitcher of water at the mouth of the cave. And he took the potsherd which was written, and he knocked and went his way, and did not talk to him, by the commandment of the old man. (f. 56 a) And here the lord Daniel read the writing of the old man, and gave him what he needed. But on one of the days he found the tablet written thus: "Bring thou at once."

The continuation of this tale is on leaves which have disappeared from the MS. Its Greek text will be found immediately after that of Eulogios, in the *Bibliothèque Hagiographe Orientale*, Editée par LÉON CLUGNET, Vol. I. It is entitled Περὶ Ἀναστασίας τῆς Πατρικίας, Anastasie la Patrice, and relates how the hermit's disciple found him ill with a fever from which he died; and how when they laid the body out for burial, it was recognized to be that of a woman, who in her youth had fled from the attentions of the Emperor Justinian; and had lived for twenty-eight years disguised in the desert; although both the Emperor and the Archbishop sent many a great man to search for her.

GLOSSARY

THIS list of uncommon words and forms in the Palestinian dialect includes all those found in No. VIII of Horae Semiticae, i.e. Codex Climaci Rescriptus, and those also in the present volume. I think that it will be found more convenient to have the two together in place of furnishing each book with a separate glossary. As I do not wish to intrude on the province of the lexicographer, nor to do my sister's work a second time, I have rigidly excluded all words already found in the Thesaurus Syriacus of Dr Payne Smith; and have given very few of those in Mrs Gibson's Glossary to No. VI *Studia Sinaitica*, or in Dr Friedrich Schulthess's *Lexicon Syropalaestinum*. The plan on which I have constructed it is the same as Mrs Gibson's; but I have preferred to give the *ipsissima verba* of the Greek text, where the Syriac is translated from a portion of Holy Writ as represented in No. VIII, or from the Greek text of the Forty Martyrs in Combefis or of Eulogios the Stone Cutter in Clugnet's text.

My readers can try to remember for themselves what is the first person singular indicative present of each verb; the nominative singular of each noun, and the nominative singular masculine of each adjective. It will not hurt them to do so; and will save me no little trouble

I trust that they will find a compensating advantage by seeing at a glance which words of the often familiar Greek text of the Scriptures correspond to the Syriac ones.

A peculiarity of this dialect is the frequent insertion of a *yod* between the initial *mim* of a participle and its first radical letter; sometimes also between the *alaf* and the *tau* of the prefix to verbs, for example, in ܐܝܬܥܒܕ. This must have been adopted to indicate a peculiarity of pronunciation; and it is so very common that quite probably I may have omitted to notice some cases of it. The forms which insert a *yod* between the second and third radicals of the participles, preterite (Peal) indicative, and imperative of verbs, of which my sister says she has given few examples, because it is so common in the eleventh century text of the Lectionaries, hardly occur in these earlier texts of the fifth and sixth centuries. Possibly this *yod* crept into the dialect after Arabic had superseded it on the lips of educated people; when it was being more and more relegated to the homes of the obscure peasantry.

ܐ

ܐܒ ܕܐܒܐܝ Matt. **26**. 29. τοῦ Πατρός μου (VIII p. 56, col. 3).

ܐܒܕ ✠ ܘܬܘܒܕ Deut. **7**. 23. καὶ ἀπολεῖς (VIII p. 16, col. 4).

ܐܒܠ ܬܬܐܒܠ Jer. **12**. 4. πενθήσει (VIII p. 34, col. 2).

ܐܒܢܥܙܪ 1 Sam. **4**. 1. Ἀβενέζερ Ebenezer (VIII p. 22, col. 2).

ܐܓܪܝܦܣ Acts **25**. 13. Ἀγρίππας (VIII p. 92, col. 2). Acts **25**. 22 (VIII p. 94, col. 1).

ܐܓܘܢܐ = ܒܐܓܘܢܗ ἐν τῷ ἀγῶνι (VIII p. 198, col. 3).

ܠܐܓܘܢܐ εἰς τὸν ἀγῶνα (p. 198, col. 4).

ܐܘܟܠܘܣ Matt. **26**. 47. ὄχλος (VIII p. 58, col. 3).

ܐܘܢܛܘܣ 1 Cor. **14**. 25. Οὕτως (VIII p. 126, col. 1). Gal. **3**. 21 (VIII p. 148, col. 1).

ܐܘܢܣܝܡܘܣ Col. **4**. 9. Ὀνησίμῳ (VIII p. 164, col. 1).

ܕܐܘܢܣܝܦܘܪܘܣ 2 Tim. **1**. 16. τῷ Ὀνησιφόρῳ (VIII p. 172, col. 3).

ܐܘܪܩܠܝܘܢ = ܐܘܪܩܘܠܝܘܢ Acts **27**. 14. Εὐρακύλων (VIII p. 100, col. 1).

ܐܙܠ ܬܐܙܠ Acts **25**. 12. πορεύσῃ (VIII p. 92, col. 2). ܘܢܝܙܠ 2 Cor. **5**. 8. καὶ ἐνδημῆσαι (VIII p. 138, col. 3). ܘܝܙܠܘܢ and they should go (VIII p. 190, col. 3). ܕܝܙܠܘܢ that they should go (idem). ܢܐܙܠ Cod. ܢܐܙܠܘܢ *bis* Eulogios let us go (IX p. 55, col. 2). ܘܢܐܙܠ that he might go (IX p. 60, col. 1).

ܐܙܢ ܒܡܘܙܢܝܐ Job **6**. 2. ἐν ζυγῷ (VIII p. 18, col. 1).

ܘܕܐܟܝܐܝܩܘܣ 1 Cor. **16**. 17. καὶ Ἀχαϊκοῦ (VIII p. 134, col. 1).

ܐܚܪ ܒܚܪܝܗܘܢ Micah **4**. 1. ἐπ' ἐσχάτων (VIII p. 2, col. 3). ܘܒܬܪ ܒܚܪܘܗܝ Joel **2**. 20. καὶ τὰ ὀπίσω αὐτοῦ (VIII p. 8, col. 2). ܕܚܪܝܝܐ 1 Cor. **4**. 9. ἐσχάτους (VIII

p. 120, col. 2). ܠܒܣܬܪܝ Eulogios behind me (IX p. 74, col. 1).

ܐܝܛܐ + = ܐܝܛܐ εἶτα then (VIII p. 192, col. 1).

ܐܬܐ ܐܝܬܝܬܘܢ Acts 19. 37. ἠγάγετε (VIII p. 84, col. 3).

ܕܝܬܝܘܢ Acts 25. 17. ἀχθῆναι (VIII p. 92, col. 4).

ܐܠܝܬ Martyrs Elesius Ἠλέσιος (IX p. 21, col. 2).

ܐܘܟܘܢ Eulogios Οὐκοῦν (IX p. 59, col. 2).

ܐܘܪ ܒܐܐܘܪܐ through the air (VIII p. 196, col. 3).

ܐܟܐܝܐ 2 Cor. 1. 1. τῇ Ἀχαΐᾳ (VIII p. 134, col. 4).

ܐܟܠ ܢܝܟܘܠ 1 Cor. 15. 32. φάγωμεν (VIII p. 130, col. 3). ܐܟܘܠ Eulogios γεύσομαι (IX p. 62, col. 2). ܡܝܟܠ Acts 27. 21. σῖτος (VIII p. 100, col. 3).

ܘܐܠܟܣܝܟܪܝܛܣ Eulogios καὶ Λεξικραίτης (IX p. 76, col. 1).

ܐܟܣܢܝܝܢ Eulogios ξένους (IX p. 69, col. 2). ܠܐܟܣܢܝܝܢ Eulogios τοῖς ξένοις (idem).

ܐܠܘܪܝܩܘܢ Rom. 15. 19. τοῦ Ἰλλυρικοῦ (VIII p. 114, col. 4).

ܐܠܘܬ + = ܐܠܘ ܐܝܬ? Phil. 2. 17. Ἀλλὰ εἰ (VIII p. 162, col. 2).

ܘܐܠܝܬܐ Lev. 8. 25. καὶ τὴν ὀσφύν (VIII p. 4, col. 2).

ܐܠܟܣܢܕܪܝܢܐܝ Acts 27. 6. Ἀλεξανδρινόν (VIII p. 98, col. 2).

ܐܠܟܣܢܕܪܝܢܝ Eulogios (idem) (IX p. 73, col. 1).

ܐܠܣܐ Acts 27. 8. Ἀλάσσα, Λασαία (VIII p. 98, col. 2).

ܐܠܝ ܘܐܠܝܢ = ܘܐܠܐܝܢ Afel. Jer. 12. 5. καὶ ἐκλύουσιν (VIII p. 34, col. 3).

ܐܠܦ ܬܠܦܘܢ 1 Cor. 4. 6. μάθητε (VIII p. 120, col. 1).

ܐܡܟܣܐ 1 Sam. 6. 7. ἅμαξαν (VIII p. 24, col. 1).

ܐܡ ܕܐܡܐܝ Gal. 1. 15. μητρός μου (VIII p. 146, col. 2).

ܐܡܢ ܬܗܝܡܢܝܢ Jer. 12. 6. πιστεύσῃς (VIII p. 34, col. 3).

ܐܡܪ ܕܬܐܡܘܪ Eulogios [until] thou say (IX p. 60, col. 1).

ܘܬܝܡܘܪ Lev. 12. 2. καὶ ἐρεῖς (VIII p. 6, col. 2).

ܐܡܪ ܐܡܪ̈ܝܐ Matt. **26**. 31. τὰ πρόβατα (VIII p. 56, col. 4).
ܐܢܒܘܒܐ 1 Cor. **14**. 7. αὐλός (VIII p. 124, col. 2). ܒܐܢܒܘܒܐ 1 Cor. **14**. 7. τὸ αὐλούμενον (VIII p. 124 col. 2).
ܐܢܬܘܦܛܝܢ Acts **19**. 38. ἀνθύπατοι (VIII p. 84, col. 3
ܒܐܢܛܝܘܟܝܐ 2 Tim. **3**. 11. ἐν Ἀντιοχείᾳ (VIII p. 174, col. 3).
ܐܢܬܝܐ Martyrs destiny or profit Heb. אנה (IX p. 26, col. 2). whither? Arab. انى ܥܠ ܐܢܬܝܐ ܕܢܦܫܗ περὶ ψυχῆς. Cf. ܐܢܬܝܗ (IX p. 2, col. 2).
ܕܐܢܣܛܣܝܣ Rubric τῆς Ἀναστάσεως (VIII p. 22, col. 2).

ܐܢܬܬܐ ܕܢܫܝܢ = ܕܢܫܝܢ of women (VIII p. 200, col. 4).
ܠܐܣܘܣ Acts **20**. 13. ἐπὶ τὴν Ἄσσον (VIII p. 86, col. 4).
ܕܐܣܩܝܛܝܣ = ܕܐܣܩܝܛܝܣ Eulogios τῆς Σκήτεως (IX p. 54, col. 2). ܠܐܣܩܝܛܝܣ εἰς Σκήτην (IX p. 55, col. 1).

ܐܣܪ ܒܐܣܘܪ̈ܝܐ Philemon 13. ἐν τοῖς δεσμοῖς (VIII p. 178, col. 1).
ܒܐܘܦܘܡ̈ܢܝܡܛܐ Martyrs τὰ ὑπομνήματα (IX p. 53, col. 1).
ܐܦܦܪܣ Col. **4**. 12. Ἐπαφρᾶς (VIII p. 164, col. 3). ܐܦܦܪܣ Philemon 23 (VIII p. 178, col. 2).

ܦܝܣ ܝܗܒ ܐܦܣܘ Acts **25**. 8. ἀπολογουμένου (VIII p. 90, col. 4).
ܐܦ ܐܢ = ܐܦܢ Also if (VIII p. 194, col. 1).
ܒܐܦܩ 1 Sam. **4**. 1. ἐν Ἀφέκ (VIII p. 22, col. 2).
ܐܦܦܪܘܕܝܛܘܣ Phil. **2**. 25. Ἐπαφρόδιτον (VIII p. 162, col. 4).
ܐܦܪܟܘܣ Eulogios ἔπαρχος (IX p. 66, col. 2). ܐܦܪܟܐ ἔπαρχος (IX p. 72, col. 1).
ܐܦܪܟܝܐ ἐπαρχία (IX p. 66, col. 2).
ܐܩܘܠܘܬܝܐ Rubric to 1 Sam. **4**. 1—6[a]. Ἀκολουθία (VIII p. 22, col. 2).
ܐܩܪܘܢ = ܥܩܪܘܢ 1 Sam. **6**. 17. τῆς Ἀκκαρὼν Ekron (VIII p. 26, col. 3).
ܐܪܓܘܒ 1 Sam. **6**. 8, 11 ἐργάβ, βερεχθάν (VIII p. 24, cols. 2, 4).

ܘܐܪܡܘܓܢܝܣ 2 Tim. **1**. 15. *καὶ Ἑρμογένης* (VIII p. 172, col. 3).

ܐܪܡܝܣ Jeremiah (VIII p. 196, col. 2).

ܐܪܡܬܝ، ܕܨܘܦܝܡ 1 Sam. **1**. 1. Ἀρμαθάιμ Σειφὰ Ἀριμαθάια? (VIII p. 32, col. 4).

ܐܪܝܣܛܪܟܘܣ Col. **4**. 10. Ἀρίσταρχος (VIII p. 164, col. 2). Philemon 24 (VIII p. 178, col. 4).

ܐܪܟܠܐܘܣ = ܐܪܟܐܠܐܘܣ Matt. **2**. 22. Ἀρχέλαος (VIII p. 40, col. 2).

ܐܪܥܐ ܠܪܥ Martyrs *κατωτέρω* (IX p. 21, col. 2). Acts **20**. 9. *κάτω* (VIII p. 86, col. 3).

ܕܐܝܫܝ Rom. **15**. 12. *τοῦ Ἰεσσαὶ* (VIII p. 114, col. 1).

ܐܫܥܝܐܣ idem Ἡσαΐας (idem).

ܐܪܣ ܐܬܐܪܣܬ = ܐܬܗܪܣܬ Matt. **1**. 18. *μνηστευθείσης* (VIII p. 36, col. 1).

ܐܬܐ ܕܡܐܬܐܢ 2 Tim. **3**. 7. *ἐλθεῖν* (VIII p. 174, col. 2; p. 200, col. 2).

ܐܬܠܝܛܐ 2 Tim. **2**. 5. *ἀθλητής* (VIII p. 198, col. 3). ܐܬܠܝܛ ♣

ܒ

ܒܪ ܒܪܘܝܐ Acts **20**. 4. Βεροιαῖος (VIII p. 86, col. 1).

ܒܘܢ ܒܘܢܘ Job **6**. 30. *σύνεσις* (VIII p. 28, col. 3).

ܒܘܡܘܣܝܗܘܢ Deut. **7**. 5. *τοὺς βωμοὺς αὐτῶν* (VIII p. 12, col. 4).

ܒܘܓܝܐ Eulogios lamp (IX p. 57, col. 1).

ܒܝܐ Martyrs *βία* (IX p. 18, col. 2).

ܒܠܡܝܢ Martyrs *βλεμμύων* (IX p. 27, col. 2). ܒܠܡܐܝܢ idem (IX p. 29 col. 2).

ܒܠܝܐܪ 2 Cor. **6**. 15. Βελίαρ (VIII p. 140, col. 4).

ܒܣܪ ܕܗܘܦ ܒܣܪܐܬ Rom. **8**. 12. *κατὰ σάρκα* (VIII p. 110, col. 2)

ܒܥܐ ܒܥܝܢ 1 Cor. **14**. 35. θέλουσιν *fem.* (VIII p. 126, col. 4). ܒܥܘܢܝܐ Acts **25**. 20. ζήτησιν (VIII p. 94, col. 1).

ܒܩܪ ܒܩܘܪܬܐ Deut. **7**. 13. τὰ βουκόλια (VIII p. 14, col. 4).

ܒܪ ܕܒܪܘ Rom. **8**. 15. υἱοθεσίας (VIII p. 110, col. 3).
ܒܪ̈ܝܐ, Gal. **4**. 19. τέκνα μου (VIII p. 150, col. 2).
ܕܒܪܢܒܐܣ Col. **4**. 10. Βαρνάβα *gen.* (VIII p. 164, col. 2).

ܒܪܐ ܐܒܪܐ 2 Cor. **2**. 5. ἐπιβαρῶ (VIII p. 136, col. 3).
ܕܒܪܐ ܚܠܝܢ 2 Cor. **5**. 4. βαρούμενοι (VIII p. 138, col. 2).

ܒܫܠ ܒܫܘܠ Eulogios ἑψητόν (IX p. 68, col. 1).

ܒܬܠ ܒܬܠܬܐ = ܒ̈ܬܘܠܬܐ virgins? (VIII p. 192, col. 3).

ܒܬܪ ܕܒܬܪܗ Acts **25**. 27. τὰς κατ' αὐτοῦ (αἰτίας) (VIII p. 94, col. 4).

ܓ

ܓܐܝܘܣ 1 Cor. **1**. 14. Γάϊος (VIII p. 116, col. 4).

ܓܒ ܓܒ παρά beside cf. جنب Arab. side (IX p. 83, col. 1).
ܓܒܘܢ Martyrs παρ' ὑμῖν (IX p. 50, col. 1).
ܓܒܗ 1 Sam. **6**. 14. παρ' αὐτῇ (VIII p. 26, col. 1).
ܡܢ ܓܒܗ Martyrs ἐξ αὐτοῦ (IX p. 20, col. 2).

ܓܘܒ ܕܝܬܠ ܐܓܘܒ Acts **19**. 40. ἀποδοῦναι λόγον (VIII p. 84, col. 4).

ܓܘܪ Arab. جوز ܓܪܘ = ܓܐܪܘ Martyrs περάσαντες transeuntes (IX p. 27, col. 2).

ܒܓܬܪܒܝ Martyrs εἰς Γεθραββί in Gethrabbi (IX p. 5, col. 1).
ܓܠܘܣܘܩܘܡܘܣܐ = ܓܠܘܣܩܘܡܘܣܐ John **13**. 29. γλωσσόκομον (VIII p. 80, col. 4).

ܓܘܪܢܐ ✤ Acts **27**. 17. Σύρτιν (VIII p. 100, col. 2).

ܓܦ ܥܠ ܓܦ = ܥܠ ܓܦܐ Martyrs πλησίον (IX p. 53, col. 2). ܘܓܦ ܠܗ Acts 20. 10. καὶ συνπεριλαβὼν (αὐτόν) (VIII p. 86, col. 3).

ܕ

ܕܒܪ ܕܒܘܪܝܬܐ Deut. 7. 20. τὰς σφηκίας (VIII p. 16, col. 2).
ܕܒܪܗܘܢ = ܕܒܘܪܗܘܢ Martyrs ἡ διαγωγὴ αὐτῶν discipline (IX p. 3, col. 1).

ܕܓܠ ܡܕܓܠ deceive (VIII p. 190, col. 2).

ܕܘܠܣ Dulas Δουλᾶς (IX p. 51, col. 1).

ܕܘܢ ܡܕܝܢܬܐ = ܡܕܝܢܬܐ (VIII p. 190, cols. 3, 4).

ܕܘܪ ܕܐܝܪܐ go about (VIII p. 194, col. 2).

ܕܝܐܟܪܝܣܝܣ Martyrs διάκρισις (IX p. 21, col. 2).

ܕܝܡܝܛܪܝܣ = ܕܝܡܝܛܪܝܘܣ Acts 19. 38. Δημήτριος (VIII p. 84, col. 3).

ܕܝܡܣ Col. 4. 14. Δημᾶς (VIII p. 164, col. 4).

ܕܟܪ ܕܟܪ remembering *sing.* (VIII p. 200, col. 3). ܕܟܪܝܢ remembering *plur.* (VIII p. 200, col. 1). ܬܕܟܪ Deut. 7. 18. μνησθήσῃ (VIII p. 16, col. 2). ܐܬܕܟܪ Ps. 131. 1. Μνήσθητι (VIII p. 78, col. 1).

ܕܪ ܕܕܪܘܡܐ Martyrs ὁ νότος Austro (IX p. 28, col. 2).

ܗ

ܗܘܐ ܕܗܘܐܝ 1 Sam. 2. 22. αἵτινες ἦσαν (VIII p. 20, col. 2). ܕܗܘܐܝܢ Martyrs idem (IX p. 4, col. 1). ܗܘܝ ܐܙܠܝܢ 1 Sam. 6. 12. ἐπορεύοντο (VIII p. 24, col. 4).
ܘܗܘܝ ܠܐܝܐܝܢ 1 Sam. 6. 12. καὶ ἐκοπίων (VIII p. 24, col. 4).

ܗܘܠܘܓܝ Eulogios Εὐλόγιε *vocative* (IX p. 77, col. 2).

ܗܘܠܘܣ 1 Cor. **15**. 29. ὅλως (VIII p. 130, col. 2). ܗܘܠܘܣ Eulogios ὄντως (IX p. 69, col. 2).

ܘܗܘܣܘܦܘܣ Heb. **9**. 19. καὶ ὑσσώπου (VIII p. 184, col. 4).

ܒܗܝܕܐ Matt. **21**. 24, 27. ἐν ποίᾳ (VIII p. 42, cols. 1, 3).

ܗܠܝܟܢ Gal. **6**. 11. πηλίκοις (VIII p. 154, col. 4).

ܗܠܟ ܗܠܟܢܢ Eph. **2**. 3. ἀνεστράφημεν (VIII p. 156, col. 3).

ܗܠܡܝܢܐ Martyrs τὸν λιμένα (IX p. 8, col. 1).

ܗܡܙܕܐ = ܐܡܙܕܐ Job **6**. 2. ὁμοθυμαδόν (VIII p. 18, col. 1).

ܗܢܐ ܠܗܢܝܬܗ Eulogios τὰ πρὸς σωτηρίαν (IX p. 58, col. 1). ܗܢܝܬܗ Martyrs ὠφελείας *gen.* (IX p. 2, col. 2); cf. ܐܢܝܬܐ (IX p. 26, col. 2). ܐܗܢܝ Cod. ܐܗܢܝ Aphel. profited (VIII p. 198, col. 2).

ܕܗܦܛܝܐ Eulogios τῆς ὑπατείας (IX p. 67, col. 1).

ܗܦܛܝܘܣ Eulogios Hephitios (IX p. 76, col. 1).

ܗܦܟ ܗܦܘܟܝ Gal. **1**. 13. τὴν ἐμὴν ἀναστροφήν (VIII p. 146, col. 1).

ܗܦܪܟܝܘܣ Acts **25**. 1. τῇ ἐπαρχείῳ (VIII p. 90, col. 2).

ܗܪܦܐ arms (VIII p. 190, col. 1).

ܘܙ ܒܘܙ Acts **26**. 26. ἐν γωνίᾳ (VIII p. 96, col. 2).

ܘܠܒ ܕܠܐ ܘܠܒ Deut. **6**. 8. ἀσάλευτον (VIII p. 8, col. 4).

ܘܫܪ ܕܘܫܪܝ Mark **15**. 17. πορφύραν (VIII p. 76, col. 4).

ܘܢ ܒܘܢܝܐ 2 Cor. **6**. 7. διὰ τῶν ὅπλων (VIII p. 140, col. 2).

ܘܟܐ ܠܗܠܝܢ ✠ ܕܙܟܘ 2 Peter **1**. 1. τοῖς λαχοῦσιν (VIII p. 186, col. 1).

ܘܡܦ ܘܡܦ Acts **19**. 36. ἀναντιρρήτων (VIII p. 84, col. 3).

ܙܪܥ ܙܪܥܢܝܐ 1 Cor. **15**. 37, 38. σπερμάτων (VIII pp. 130, col. 4; 132, col. 1).

ܚ

ܚܓܠ ܘܚܘܓܠܬ Rom. 15. 19. *καὶ κύκλῳ* (VIII p. 114, col. 1).

ܚܓܪ ܚܓܪܬܝ Job 6. 30. Arab. حنجر *ὁ λάρυγξ μου* (VIII p. 28, col. 3).

ܚܕܐ ܚܕܐ 2 Cor. 2. 3. *χαίρειν* (VIII p. 136, col. 2).
ܘܚܕܕܝܐ and rejoicings (VIII p. 194, col. 3). ܡܬܚܕܝܐ joyful (idem).

ܚܘܐ ܠܚܘܝܐ Ex. 4. 17. *εἰς ὄφιν* (VIII p. 2, col. 1).

ܚܘܒ ܚܝܐܒ Acts 25. 15. *καταδίκην* (VIII p. 92, col. 3).
ܬܬܚܝܐܒ Acts 19. 40. *ἐγκαλεῖσθαι* (VIII p. 84, col. 4). ܠܚܘܒ 2 Cor. 7. 3. *πρὸς κατάκρισιν* (VIII p. 142, col. 2). ܕܚܝܐܒ Gal. 5. 3. *ὅτι ὀφειλέτης* (VIII p. 152, col. 2).

ܚܘܣ ܕܗܘܢ ܚܐܣ 2 Cor. 1. 23. *ὅτι φειδόμενος* (VIII p. 136, col. 1).
ܚܘܦܢܝ 1 Sam. 4. 4. *Ὀφνεί* (VIII p. 22, col. 4).

ܚܙܐ ܒܡܚܙܝ 1 Cor. 13. 12. *δι᾽ ἐσόπτρου* (VIII p. 122, col. 3).

ܚܙܢ ܠܚܙܢܐ Martyrs *εἰς τὸ ὀχύρωμα* (IX p. 4, col. 2).

ܚܝܐ ܕܡܚܝܐ Rom. 4. 17. *τοῦ ζωοποιοῦντος* (VIII p. 102, col. 1). ܘܬܚܝܘܢ 2 Cor. 7. 3. *καὶ συνζῆν* (VIII p. 142, col. 3).

ܚܝܠ ܚܘܠܝܐ Job 6. 23. *δυναστῶν* (VIII p. 28, col. 2).

ܚܠܡ ܒܚܠܡܝ̈ܐ Job 7. 14. *ἐνυπνίοις* (VIII p. 30, col. 3).
ܚܠܩܢܐ 1 Sam. 1. 1. *Ἐλκανά* (VIII p. 32, col. 4).

ܚܠܩ ܚܠܘܩܝ Cant. 5. 3. tunica mea (VIII p. 194, col. 4).

ܚܠܦ ܠܚܠܘܦܐ Eph. 4. 14. *πρὸς τὴν μεθοδίαν* (VIII p. 158, col. 1).

ܚܠܨ ܚܠܨ stripped ܚܠܘܨܘ strip *imper.* (VIII p. 198, col. 3).

ܚܡܐ ܒܚܡܝܘ 2 Cor. 5. 7. *διὰ εἴδους* (VIII p. 138, col. 3).

ܚܢܩ ܒܚܢܩܝܢ 2 Cor. **6**. 4. *ἐν ἀνάγκαις* (VIII p. 140, col. 1).

ܚܪܒ ܡܚܘܪܒܐ is fighting (VIII p. 198, col. 2).

ܚܪܪ ܒܚܪܘܪܝܬܐ Gal. **5**. 1. *Τῇ ἐλευθερίᾳ* (VIII p. 152, col. 1).

ܕܚܪܘܬܗ = ܕܚܐܪܘܬܗ of his liberty (VIII p. 200, col. 4).

ܚܪܐ ܡܚܪܬ ܐܬ Jer. **12**. 5. *παρασκευάσῃ* (VIII p. 34, col. 3).

ܚܫܠ ܡܫܚܠܬܐ = ܡܫܚܠܬܐ Acts **27**. 18. *χειμῶν* (VIII p. 100, col. 2).

ܛ

ܛܟ ܛܟܐ Philemon 15. *τάχα* (VIII p. 178, col. 2).

ܛܠܡ ܛܐܠܘܡ Eulogios *ἄδικος* (IX p. 78, col. 2).

ܘܛܝܡܬܐܘܣ Acts **20**. 4. *καὶ Τιμόθεος* (VIII p. 86, col. 1). ܘܛܝܡܬܐܘܣ 1 Thess. **1**. 1 (VIII p. 166, col. 2). 2 Thess. **1**. 1. idem (VIII p. 168, col. 3). ܕܛܝܡܬܐܘܣ Phil. **2**. 19. idem *Τιμόθεον* (VIII p. 162, col. 2).

ܛܡܥ ܛܡܥ = ܛܥܡ Acts **20**. 9. submersus est *κατενεχθεὶς* (VIII p. 86, col. 3).

ܛܦܐ ܛܦܐ Martyrs *ῥανίς* guttula (IX p. 39, col. 2).

ܛܦܚ ܛܦܚܝܐ Clappings of hands (VIII p. 194, col. 3).

ܛܪܗ ܛܪܗ Lev. **8**. 24. *κύκλῳ* (VIII p. 4, col. 2). ܘܐܛܪܗܗ Matt. **21**. 33. *καὶ περιέθηκεν* (VIII p. 44, col. 2). ܛܪܗܝܢ Matt. **23**. 15. *περιάγετε* (VIII p. 48, col. 4). Gal. **1**. 6. *μετατίθεσθε* (VIII p. 144, col. 3).

ܝ

ܝܒܠ ܐܘܒܠܘ 1 Sam. **6**. 7. *ἀπαγάγετε* (VIII p. 24, col. 2).

ܝܕ ܒܐܝܕܝܢ 1 Cor. **4**. 12. *ταῖς ἰδίαις χερσίν (ἡμῶν)* (VIII p. 120, col. 3). ܐܝܕܝܐ Eulogios *τῶν χειρῶν* (IX p. 63, col. 2).

ܝܕܥ ܐܝܕܥܝܢ Matt. **27**. 65. *οἴδατε* (VIII p. 66, col. 1). ܬܬܝܕܥܘܢ Martyrs *θεωροῦντο* conspiciunt (IX p. 29, col. 1).

ܝܗܒ ܘܐܝܗܒ Matt. **26**. 26. *καὶ δούς* (VIII p. 56, col. 2). ܘܐܝܗܒܘ ܫܪܫܝܗܘܢ Jer. **12**. 2. *καὶ ἐριζώθησαν* (VIII p. 34, col. 1).

ܡܗ̈ܒܝܢ corrige ܡܬ̈ܒܝܢ 2 Cor. **5**. 6. *ἐνδημοῦντες* (VIII p. 138, col. 2). ܡܗ̈ܒܝܢ 2 Cor. **5**. 9. *ἐκδημοῦντες* (VIII p. 138, col. 3).

ܝܘܣܛܝܢܝܢܘܣ = ܝܘܣܛܝܢܢܘܣ Ἰουστινιανός Justinian (IX p. 76, col. 1).

ܝܡܐ ܝܡܐܢܐ = ܝܡܐ ܐܢܐ Job **7**. 12. *θάλασσα* (VIII p. 30, col. 2).

ܠܝܥܩܘܒܘܣ = ܠܝܥܩܘܒܘܣ 1 Cor. **14**. 7. Ἰακώβῳ (VIII p. 128, col. 3). ܠܝܥܩܘܒܣ Gal. **1**. 19. Ἰάκωβον (VIII p. 146, col. 3).

ܝܩܢ ܘܐܬܝܩܢܘܢ Arab. يَقِنَ Rom. **4**. 21. *καὶ πληροφορηθείς* (VIII p. 102, col. 2). ܘܝܩܢܬ Eulogios *ἐγνώρισα* (IX p. 71, col. 2).

ܝܩܪ ܝܩܪܝܐ Gal. **6**. 2. *τὰ βάρη* (VIII p. 154, col. 2).

ܡܝܩܪܐ honoured *fem.* (VIII p. 194, col. 2).

ܕܒܝܪܦܘܠܝܣ Col. **4**. 13. *τῶν ἐν Ἱεραπόλει* (VIII p. 164, col. 4).

ܝܪܡܐܝܠ 1 Sam. **1**. 1. Ἰερεμεήλ (VIII p. 32, col. 4).

ܝܪܬ ܒܢ̈ܝ ܝܪܘܬܬܗ Rom. **8**. 17. *κληρονόμοι.* ܝܪ̈ܘܬܘ idem (VIII p. 110, col. 3).

ܝܫܢ ܒܝܫܢܬܐ = ܒܝܫܢܬܐ in sleep (VIII p. 200, col. 4).

ܝܬܪܘ Exod. **4**. 18. Ἰοθόρ (VIII p. 2, col. 1).

ܝܫܪ ܘܒܝܫܝܪܘ Eph. **4**. 24. *καὶ ὁσιότητι* (VIII p. 158, col. 4).

ܝܬܪ ܡܝܬܪ̈ܬܐ Eulogios ἀρετὰς (IX p. 59, col. 1). ܡܝܬܪܬܐ = ܡܬܪܬܐ τὴν ἀρετήν (IX p. 62, col. 1). ܡܝܬܪ 1 Cor. 15. 41. διαφέρει (VIII p. 132, col. 2).

ܟ

ܟܐܐ ܟܘܝܘܟܘܢ Job 6. 26. ὁ ἔλεγχος ὑμῶν (VIII p. 28, col. 2).

ܟܠܘ ܟܠܘܡ Job 6. 22. μή τι (VIII p. 28, col. 2). Job 6. 24. εἴ τι (idem). ܠܟܠܘܡ 1 Cor. 14. 10. οὐδέν (VIII p. 124, col. 3).

ܟܘܫܐܝ Eulogios Αἰθίοπος (IX p. 67, col. 1).

ܘܒܟܘܪܝܒ καὶ ἐν Χωρήβ (IX p. 5, col. 1).

ܟܠܘܐܝܣ = ܟܠܐܐ 1 Cor. 1. 11. Χλόη (VIII p. 116, col. 2).

ܟܕܘ ܡܢ ܟܕܘ = ܡܢ ܟܕܘ Matt. 26. 29. ἀπ' ἄρτι (VIII p. 56, col. 3).

ܠܚܬܝܐ Deut. 7. 1. τὸν Χατταῖον (VIII p. 12, col. 3).

ܟܠܡܝܣܐ = ܟܠܡܝܣܐ Matt. 27. 31. τὴν χλαμύδα (VIII p. 62, col. 2). ܟܠܡܝܣ Mark 15. 17. χλαμύδα (VIII p. 76, col. 4).

ܟܠ ܟܘܠܠܝܗ Acts 27. 19. τὰς σκευὰς τοῦ [πλοίου] (VIII p. 100, col. 2). ܕܟܠܠ 2 Cor. 5. 5. ὁ κατεργασάμενος (VIII p. 138, col. 2).

ܟܢܐ ܘܟܢܘܐ ܠܐ ܬܪܥ sic in Cod. 2 Tim. 1. 10. καὶ ἀφθαρσίαν (VIII p. 172, col. 1). lege fortasse ܟܝܢܐ φύσις (Duensing).

ܟܡܢ ܟܡܝܢ Acts 25. 3. ἐνέδρα (VIII p. 90, col. 3).

ܟܢܫ ܟܢܝܫܬܐ = ܟܢܫܬܐ Church (VIII p. 196, col. 2). ܟܢܘܫܐ Acts 19. 40. τῆς συστροφῆς (VIII p. 84, col. 4).

ܟܥܟ̈ܬܝܢ παξαμάδια cakes (IX p. 68, col. 1).

ܟܦܠ ܟܦܘܠܐ Is. 40. 2. διπλᾶ (VIII p. 32, col. 2).

ܟܬܪ ܕܢܬܟܬܪ Eulogios (ἔχομεν) μεῖναι (IX p. 55, col. 1).

ܟܬܫ ܬܟܬܫܘܬܟܘܢ Cf. Eph. 6. 12. ὑμῖν ἡ πάλη (VIII p. 198, col. 4).

ܠ

ܠܐܐ ܘܐܠܝܢ = ܘܐܠܐܝܢ Jer. 12. 5. καὶ ἐκλύουσιν (VIII p. 34, col. 3). ܠܐܝܢ 1 Sam. 6. 12. ἐκοπίων (VIII p. 24, col. 4).

ܠܐܝ = ܠܗܝ ܒܠܗܘܐܢ 2 Cor. 6. 5. ἐν κόποις (VIII p. 140, col. 1).

ܠܒܝܒ ܕܠܒܝܒܘܬܐ Eph. 1. 19. τοῦ κράτους (VIII p. 156, col. 1).

ܠܗܒ ܫܠܐܒܝܬܐ = ܫܠܗܒܝܬܐ Martyrs φλόξ (IX p. 5, col. 2).

ܠܘܩܣ Col. 4. 14. Λουκᾶς (VIII p. 164, col. 4).

ܠܘܫ = ܠܛܫ ܘܠܘܫܘܢ Micah 4. 3. καὶ κατακόψουσιν (VIII p. 2, col. 4).

ܠܚܫ ✠ܠܚܫܝܢ whispering (VIII p. 200, col. 3).

ܘܠܘ̈ܝܝ 1 Sam. 6. 15. καὶ οἱ Λευεῖται (VIII p. 26, col. 1).

ܠܘ̈ܪܝ Acts 19. 38. libri? (VIII p. 84, col. 3).

ܕܠܘܩܝܐ Acts 27. 5. τῆς Λυκίας (VIII p. 98, col. 1).

ܠܘܟ ܡܠܘܟܐ Cant. 5. 3. μολύνω (VIII p. 194, col. 4). ܡܠܘܟ idem (VIII p. 196, col. 2).

ܠܘܚܝܬܐ Luhith (VIII p. 192, col. 3).

ܠܡܝܢܐ Acts 27. 12. λιμήν (VIII p. 98, col. 4). ܠܝ̈ܡܝܢܝܐ Acts 27. 8. Λιμένας (VIII p. 98, col. 2).

ܠܛܦ ܡܘܠܛܦܝ Eulogios πηρίον (IX p. 67, col. 2).

ܠܘܝ ܡܠܘܝܐ Martyrs ἐρρωμένους (IX p 6, col. 2).

ܡ

ܡܐܐ ܡܐܐܬܐ = 100 (VIII p. 190, col. 2). ܡܐܬܐ idem (VIII p. 192, col. 1).

ܡܚܐ ܒܡܚܐܘܢ 2 Cor. **6**. 5. ἐν πληγαῖς (VIII p. 140, col. 1).

ܡܛܢܘܝܐ Eulogios μετάνοια (IX p. 58, cols. 1, 2).

ܠܡܝܛܝܠܝܢܐ Cod. ܠܡܝܛܠܝܢܐ Acts **20**. 14. εἰς Μιτυλήνην (VIII p. 86, col. 4).

ܘܡܠܢ and ink καὶ μέλαν (VIII p. 192, col. 4).

ܠܡܝܪܐ Acts **27**. 5. Μύῤῥα (VIII p. 98, col. 1).

ܡܝܟܐܘܣ Rubric to Micah **4**. Μιχαίου (VIII p. 2, col. 3).

ܡܟܟ ܘܡܟܟܟ Eulogios καὶ ἐταπείνωσεν (IX p. 81, col. 2).

ܡܠܐ ܡܢ ܡܐܘܠܐ Job **7**. 5. ἀπὸ ἰχῶρος (VIII p. 30, col. 1). ܐܬܡܠܐܢ Acts **24**. 27. πληρωθείσης (VIII p. 90, col. 1). ܘܡܡܘܠܐ܇ 1 Thess. **1**. 5. καὶ πληροφορίᾳ (VIII p. 166, col. 3). ܡܠܝܢ Jer. **12**. 6. ἐπισυνήχθησαν (VIII p. 34, col. 3).

ܡܠܝ ܘܕܡܘܠܝܢ et perfectus καὶ τέλειος (IX p. 21, col. 2).

ܡܠܠ ܡܠܬܐ word (VIII p. 192, col. 1; p. 200, col. 2). ܡ̈ܠܐ Deut. **6**. 6. words (VIII p. 8, col. 4; p. 192, col. 2).

ܕܡܠܟܝܣܕܩ Heb. **7**. 15. Μελχισεδέκ (VIII p. 182, col. 1).

ܡܘܡܢܐ = ܡܡܘܢܐ Matt. **6**. 24. μαμωνᾷ (VIII p. 200, col. 1).

ܡܢ ܡܢܟ than thou (VIII p. 190, col. 1).

ܠܡܢܘ 1 Sam. **6**. 5. ὅπως (VIII p. 24, col. 1).

ܡܣܐ ܡܣܐܬܐ Mark **1**. 27. τοῖς ἀκαθάρτοις (VIII p. 70, col. 4).

ܡܪܐ ܡܪ̈ܐܝܢ 2 Cor. **1**. 24. κυριεύομεν (VIII p. 136, col. 1).

ܘܡܪܘ Eph. **1**. 21. καὶ κυριότητος (VIII p. 156, col. 1).

ܡܪܛܘܪ̈ܝܐ μάρτυρες (IX p. 8, col. 2).

ܡܪܫ ܕܐܡܪܫܘ Eph. **4**. 19. ἀπηλγηκότες (VIII p. 158, col. 2).

ܡܫܚ ܕܡܫܚܐ Lev. **8**. 26. ἐξ ἐλαίου (VIII p. 4, col. 3).

ܢ

ܢܐܘܛܝܐ Martyrs τους ναύτας (IX p. 30, col. 1).

ܢܐܘܣܘܢ Martyrs ναοί (IX p. 38, col. 1).

ܢܒܐ ܡܬܢܒ̈ܝܐܢ *fem. pl.* Acts **21**. 9. προφητεύουσαι (VIII p. 88, col. 3).

ܢܒܠ ܐܬܢܒܠ = ܐܬܢܘܒܠ ✤ 2 Tim. **2**. 3. συνκακοπάθησον (VIII p. 172, col. 4).

ܢܒܥ ܬܘ̈ܒܥܝܐ Martyrs πηγαί (IX p. 13, col. 1).

ܢܓܠ ܠܡܓ̈ܠܝܢ Micah **4**. 3. εἰς δρέπανα (VIII p. 2, col. 4).

ܢܕ ܢܕܘܕ Deut. **7**. 26. προσοχθίσματι (VIII p. 18, col. 1).

ܢܘܡ ܢܐܡܝܬ Eulogios ἐκάθευδον (IX p. 73, col. 2).

ܢܘܩܛܝܪ Martyrs Ναυκράτης (IX p. 53, col. 2).

ܕܢܨܘܪܝ = ܕܢܨܪܝ Matt. **2**. 23. ὅτι Ναζωραῖος (VIII p. 40, col. 2).

ܢܚܬ ܢܚܬ goes down (VIII p. 198, col. 3). ܕܢܚܘܬ ✤ Rom. **10**. 6. καταγαγεῖν (VIII p. 112, col. 4).

ܠܢܣܘܣ Acts **27**. 26. εἰς νῆσον (VIII p. 100, col. 4).

ܢܟܣ ܠܢܟܣܬܐ Jer. **12**. 3. εἰς σφαγήν (VIII p. 34, col. 2).

ܕܢܟܣܬܗ Heb. **9**. 26. τῆς θυσίας αὐτοῦ (VIII p. 76, col. 3).

ܢܟܪ ܒܢܟܘܬ ܐܟܪܘܬܗܘܢ Eph. **4**. 18. ἄγνοιαν αὐτῶν (VIII p. 158, col. 2). ܠܐܟܪܘܬܐ 2 Tim. **3**. 7. εἰς ἐπίγνωσιν (VIII p. 174, col. 2).

ܢܣܒ ܬܣܒ take (VIII p. 192, col. 4).

ܢܥܢܥܐ = ܢܢܥܐ Matt. **23**. 23. ἡδύοσμος (VIII p. 50, col. 3).

ܢܦܠ ܢܦܠ Acts **27**. 21. Ἔδει (VIII p. 100, col. 3).

ܢܦܩ ܕܢܐܦܘܩ Acts **25**. 4. ἐκπορεύεσθαι (VIII p. 90, col. 3).

ܢܐܦܩ Eulogios προῆλθον (IX p. 70, col. 2). ܒܡܦ̈ܩܢܐ Prov. **1**. 20. ἐν ἐξόδοις (VIII p. 26, col. 4).

ܢܫܝܐ = ܢܫܐ Eph. 5. 22, 24. Αἱ γυναῖκες (VIII p. 160, col. 4).

ܢܬܘܫܐ Matt. 23. 24. κώνωπα (VIII p. 50, col. 4).

ܣ

ܣܒܩ ܣܒܩܬܢܝ = ܫܒܩܬܢܝ Matt. 27. 46. σαβαχθανεί (VIII p. 64, col. 4).

ܣܒܪ ܡܣܒܪ Phil. 2. 19, 23. Ἐλπίζω (VIII p. 162, cols. 2, 4).

ܣܓܝ ܣܓܝܐܢ Eulogios πολλὰ (IX p. 63, col. 2).

ܣܕܪ ܒܣܕܘܪܐ = ܒܣܕܪܐ 1 Sam. 4. 2. εν τῃ παρατάξει (VIII p. 22, col. 3).

ܣܘܦ ܕܣܐܦ Job 6. 15. ἐκλείπων (VIII p. 18, col. 4).

ܕܐܣܛܦܢܐ 1 Cor. 16. 17. Στεφανᾶ (VIII p. 134, col. 1).

ܘܣܝܠܘܐܢܘܣ 1 Thess. 1. 1. Σιλουανός (VIII p. 166, col. 2).

ܘܣܝܠܘܢܘܣ 2 Thess. 1. 1. (VIII p. 168, col. 3).

ܦܣܝܐܘܣ Martyrs Psoës Ψόης (IX p. 20, col. 1).

ܣܝܒ ܣܝܒ Martyrs sibennio = (intextis palmarum hastulis) ἀπὸ σιβιννίου palm-fibre (IX p. 17, col. 2).

ܣܝܦ ܣܝܦܝܗܘܢ Micah 4. 3. τὰς ῥομφαίας (VIII p. 2, col. 4).

ܣܝܡ ܣܝܡܘ 2 Cor. 7. 2. Χωρήσατε (VIII p. 142, col. 2).

ܣܝܪܛܝܣ Acts 27. 17. Σύρτιν (VIII p. 100, col. 2).

ܣܟܐ ܡܣܟܐܝܢ Matt. 24. 44. δοκεῖτε (VIII p. 52, col. 2).

ܣܟܠ ܣܟܠܝܐ Mark 2. 7. ἁμαρτίας (VIII p. 72, col. 3).

ܣܟܪ ܣܟܘܪ ܦܘܡܟ Mark 1. 25. φιμώθητι (VIII p. 70, col. 3).

✠ ܣܟܪܘ Acts 27. 17. ἐνέφραξαν (for βοηθείαις ἐχρῶντο).

ܣܠܠ ܘܣܠܘܠ Joel 2. 14. καὶ σπονδήν (VIII p. 2, col. 3).

ܐܢܐ ܡܣܬܠܠ Phil. 2. 17. σπένδομαι (VIII p. 162, col. 2).

ܣܢܐ ܕܣܢܐ ܐܢܐ ⌜ ⌝ ܕ 1 Joh. 2. 11. ὁ μισῶν (VIII p. 200, col. 4).

ܣܦܕ ܘܒܡܣܦܕܐ Joel 2. 12. καὶ ἐν κοπετῷ (VIII p. 2, col. 2).

ܣܦܪ ܣܦܪܬܗ Joel **2**. 17. τῆς κρηπῖδος (αὐτοῦ) (VIII p. 8, col. 1).

ܣܦܪܐ Heb. **9**. 19. τὸ βιβλίον (VIII p. 184, col. 4).

ܐܣܩܘܛܘܢ scutum (VIII p. 196, col. 3).

ܣܪܚ ✠ܣܪܚܢ Deut. **7**. 2. ἀφανισμῷ (VIII p. 12, col. 3).

ܕܣܪܩܝܢ, ܕܣܪܩܝܐܢ Martyrs Σαρακηνῶν of the Saracens (IX p. 4, col. 1). ܣܪܩܝܐ Saracen Ἰσμαηλίτης (IX p. 10, col. 1).

ܥ

ܥܒܕ ܐܬܥܒܕ 2 Tim. **3**. 11. ἐγένετο (VIII p. 174, col. 3). ܡܫܬܥܒܕܝܢ obedient (VIII p. 200, col. 2). ܕܥܒܕ Acts **25**. 6. Διατρίψας (VIII p. 90, col. 3). ܘܥܒܕܢ Acts **21**. 7. ἐμείναμεν (VIII p. 88, col. 2).

ܥܒܪ ܘܡܥܒܪܬܐ Acts **27**. 5. τό τε πέλαγος (διάβασις) (VIII p. 98, col. 1).

ܥܗܕ Cf. Lectionary Joh. **15**. 20, **16**. 4.

ܥܗܕ ܥܗܕܘܢ Joh. **15**. 20. μνημονεύετε (VIII p. 82, col. 1).

ܥܘܒܕܝܢܘܣ Obedianos Ὀβεδιανός (IX pp. 47, 49, col. 2).

ܥܘܠ ܥܘܠܐ Titus **2**. 14. ἀνομίας (VIII p. 38, col. 1).

ܕܥܘܟܒܪܝܢܘܢ 1 Sam. **6**. 5. τῶν μυῶν ὑμῶν (VIII p. 24, col. 1).

ܥܘܩ ܐܬܥܩܘ Eulogios ἐλυπήθη (IX p. 59, col. 1).

ܕܥܙܐ 1 Sam. **6**. 17. τῆς Γάζης (VIII p. 26, col. 3).

ܥܙܐ ܘܡܥܙܐ Deut. **7**. 8. βεβαιῶν (VIII p. 14, col. 1).

ܠܥܟܘ Acts **21**. 7. εἰς Πτολεμαΐδα (VIII p. 88, col. 2).

ܥܠ ܥܠܘܢ = ܥܠܘܬܐ 1 Sam. **6**. 15. ὁλοκαυτώσεις (VIII p. 26, col. 2).

ܥܠ ܥܠܝ Eulogios ὑπὲρ ἐμοῦ (IX p. 80, col. 1). Philemon 18. ἐμοὶ (VIII p. 178, col. 2).

ܥܡܠ ܥܒܕܝ ܥܡܠܝܬܗܘܢ 2 Cor. **1**. 24. συνεργοί (VIII p. 136, col. 1). ܡܥܡܠܘܬܐ Eph. **1**. 19. τὴν ἐνέργειαν (VIII p. 156, col. 1). ܡܫܡܫܝܠ treat with = smear (VIII p. 200, col. 2). ܐܬܡܫܘ = ܐܬܡܫܡܫܘ prepare (VIII p. 200, col. 2).

ܒܢܐ ܕܒܢܝܘܬܗ Gal. **6**. 1. *πραΰτητος* (VIII p. 154, col. 2).
ܒܢܝܘܬܗ Titus **3**. 2. *πραΰτητα* (VIII p. 176, col. 4).

ܒܟܝܐ ܒܟܝܐ Acts **20**. 3. *ἐπιβουλή* (VIII p. 86, col. 1).
ܒܒܟܝܘ Eph. **4**. 19. *ἐν πλεονεξίᾳ* (VIII p. 158, col. 3).

ܒܟܝ ܠܒܟܝܘܬܗ Heb. **9**. 26. *εἰς ἀθέτησιν* (VIII p. 76, col. 3).

ܒܟܢ ܒܘܟܢܐ Heb. **9**. 23. *Ἀνάγκη* (VIII p. 76, col. 1).
ܒܒܘܟܢܐ Philemon 14. *κατὰ ἀνάγκην* (VIII p. 178, col. 1). ܐܬܒܟܢܬ Martyrs *ἠναγκάσθην* (IX p. 20, col. 2).

ܒܪܛܠ ܘܐܒܪܛܠܐܝ Job **1**. 21. *καὶ γυμνός* (VIII p. 200, col. 1).

ܦ

ܘܦܘܡܦܝܘܣ Eulogios *καὶ Πόμπιος* (IX p. 76, col. 1).
ܠܦܘܪܩܝܘܣ Acts **24**. 27. *Πόρκιον* (VIII p. 90, col. 2).
ܘܕܦܘܪܛܘܢܛܘܣ 1 Cor. **16**. 17. *καὶ Φορτουνάτου* (VIII p. 134, col. 1).

ܦܛܪ ܦܛܪܝܩܝܘܣ Eulogios *πατρίκιος* patrician (IX p. 77, col. 1; p. 70, col. 1 *bis*).
ܘܦܪܡܘܬܝܐ 1 Cor. **14**. 3. *καὶ παραμυθίαν* (VIII p. 122, col. 4).
ܦܝܠܟܣ Acts **24**. 27. *ὁ Φῆλιξ* (VIII p. 90, col. 2).
ܦܘܢܝܩܐ Acts **27**. 12. *Φοίνικα* (VIII p. 98, col. 4).

ܦܣܩ ܐܦܣܩܘܬܐ Martyrs *ἀρεσκείαν* (IX p. 14, col. 1).
ܕܦܝܪܘܣ Acts **20**. 4. *Πύρρου* (VIII p. 86, col. 1).
ܦܪܓܘܪܝܐ Col. **4**. 11. *παρηγορία* (VIII p. 164, col. 3).
ܦܡܦܘܠܝܐ Acts **27**. 5. *Παμφυλίαν* (VIII p. 98, col. 1).

ܒܦܘܠܩܝܐ *εἰς τὴν φυλακήν* (VIII p. 190, col. 3). ܠܦܘܠܩܐ (VIII p. 192, col. 1). ܕܦܘܠܩܝܐ *τῆς φυλακῆς* (idem col. 3).

ܦܘܓܠܝܠܘܣ 2 Tim. **1.** 15. *Φύγελος* (VIII p. 172, col. 3).

ܦܝܢܣ 1 Sam. **4.** 4. *Φεινεές* Phinehas (VIII p. 22, col. 4).

ܦܡ ܦܘܡܗܐ edge = (mouth of sword) (VIII p. 196, col. 3).

ܦܘܡܗܘܢ Matt. **12.** 36. *στόματος ὑμῶν* (VIII p. 200, col. 3).

ܘܦܡܦܘܠܝܐ Acts **27.** 5. *καὶ Παμφυλίαν* (VIII p. 98, col. 1).

ܦܣܕ ܦܣܕܢ Acts **27.** 10. *ζημία* (VIII p. 98, col. 3).

ܦܣܠ ܦܣܠܘܬܗ 1 Cor. **4.** 13. *περικαθάρματα* (VIII p. 120, col. 4).

ܦܣܣ ܟܕ ܗܘ ܐܦܣܘܣ Acts **25.** 8. *ἀπολογουμένου* (VIII p. 90, col. 4).

ܐܬܪ ܠܐܦܣܘܣ Acts **25.** 16. *τόπον τε ἀπολογίας* (VIII p. 92, col. 4).

ܦܢܝ ܒܦܢܝܘ Prov. **1.** 20. *παρρησίαν* (VIII p. 26, col. 4).

ܦܢܝ ܦܢܝܢ ܒܠܐ Phil. **2.** 15. *ἄμεμπτοι* (VIII p. 162, col. 1).

ܦܩܕ ܕܦܩܘܕܝܬܗܘܢ Jer. **11.** 23. *ἐπισκέψεως* (VIII p. 34, col. 1). ܒܦܩܘܕܗ in the commandment (VIII p. 192, col. 3). ܦܩܕܘܢܝ 2 Tim. **1.** 12. *τὴν παραθήκην μου* (VIII p. 172, col. 2).

ܦܪ Eulogios ܒܦܪܬ ܦܪ ܡܢ ܝܘܡܐ: much more than a day (IX p. 62, col. 2).

ܦܪܐ Eulogios *παρά* (IX p. 79, col. 2).

ܦܪܓܡܘܣ Berghamus (VIII p. 190, col. 4).

ܦܪܝܣܩܐ 1 Cor. **16.** 19. *Πρίσκα* (VIII p. 134, col. 2).

ܦܪܚ ܦܪܚܝܐ soaring (VIII p. 196, col. 3).

ܕܦܪܢ Martyrs *ἀπὸ τῆς Φαράν* (IX p. 18, col. 2).

ܦܪܐܢܝܢ Martyrs *τῶν οἰκούντων τὴν Φαράν* (IX p. 15, col. 2). ܦܪܢܝܢ idem (IX p. 19, col. 1).

ܦܪܣ ܦܪܣܘܢܗ = ܦܘܪܣܢܗ Rom. **6.** 23. *τὰ ὀψώνια τῆς* (VIII p. 106, col. 4).

ܦܪܥ ܒܦܪܥܝ Martyrs τὸ παράπαν omnino (IX p. 3, col. 2). ܒܐܦܪܥܝ Gal. **1**. 6. ταχέως (VIII p. 144, col. 3). ܒܦܪ̈ܥܝ Phil. **2**. 19, 24. idem (VIII p. 162, col. 3, 4). 2 Thess. **2**. 2 (VIII p. 170, col. 4).

ܦܪܫ ܦܪܫܘ = ܦܪܫܘܬܐ Lev. **8**. 27, 29. ἀφαίρεμα (VIII p. 4, cols, 3, 4). ܬܦܪܫ Martyrs sejunxeris χωρίσῃς (IX p. 8, col. 1).

ܦܫܛ ܕܦܐܫܛ Martyrs ἐπεκτείνων praetendit (IX p. 5, col. 2).

ܦܬ confregit ܦܬܝܬܐ Joh. **13**. 26. τὸ ψωμίον (VIII p. 80, cols. 3, 4).

ܦܬܚ ܦܬܚܝ Cant. **5**. 2. Open (VIII p. 194, col. 4).

ܨ

ܨܒܥ ܝܨܒܥ Mark **1**. 8. βαπτίσει (VIII p. 68, col. 4).

ܨܕܩ ܘܨܕܩܘ Deut. **6**. 25. καὶ ἐλεημοσύνη (VIII p. 12, col. 2) ܨܕܩܘܢ Rom. **4**. 25. τὴν δικαίωσιν ἡμῶν (VIII p. 102, col. 3). ܡܨܛܕܩܝܢ Gal. **5**. 4. δικαιοῦσθε (VIII p. 152, col. 2).

ܨܘܚ ܨܘܚܬܐ 2 Cor. **7**. 5. μάχαι (VIII p. 142, col. 3).

ܨܝܕ ܨܐܕܗ Heb. **2**. 14. τὸ κράτος (τοῦ) (VIII p. 180, col. 3).

ܨܠ ܡܨܠܝܢ 1 Sam. **2**. 22. προσευχόμεναι (VIII p. 20, col. 2).

ܨܡܕ ܨܡܝܕ Martyrs πυκνότερον crebrius (IX p. 2, col. 2). ܨܡܝܕܐܝܬ ἀεὶ semper (IX p. 5, col. 2).

ܨܥܪ ܕܨܥܪܗ 1 Sam. **6**. 8. τῆς βασάνου (VIII p. 24, col. 2). ܕܨܥܪ̈ܐ 1 Sam. **6**. 17. idem (VIII p. 26, col. 2).

ܨܦܐ ܐܨܦܘܢ Martyrs κατασκοποὺς exploratores scouts (IX p. 29, col. 1). ܕܡܢ ܨܦܘܢܐ Joel **2**. 20. τὸν ἀπὸ βορρᾶ (VIII p. 8, col. 2).

ܩ

ܩܒܠ ܠܩܒܠܗ Acts **25**. 19. πρὸς αὐτόν (VIII p. 92, col. 4). ܢܩܒܠ Martyrs λημψόμεθα (IX p. 33, col. 1). ܩܒܠܬܗ 1 Cor. **15**. 3. παρέλαβον (αὐτόν) (VIII p. 128, col. 2).

ܩܘܕܪ Codar Κοδάρ (IX p. 5, col. 1).

ܠܩܘܒܪܢܝܛܐ Acts **27**. 11. τῷ κυβερνήτῃ (VIII p. 98, col. 3).

ܩܕܡ ܠܩܕܡܘܬܗ 1 Sam. **6**. 13. εἰς ἀπάντησιν αὐτῆς (VIII p. 26, col. 1).

ܩܘܡ ܩܝܡܬܗܘܢ 1 Cor. **15**. 42. ἡ ἀνάστασις (αὐτῶν) (VIII p. 132, col. 2).

ܩܛܝܪ Job **6**. 7. καὶ γὰρ (VIII p. 18, col. 3; p. 198, col. 1).

ܩܘܣܛܢܛܝܢܘܦܘܠܝܣ Eulogios τὸ Βυζάντιον (IX p. 66, col. 1). ܩܘܣܛܢܛܝܢܘܦܘܠܝܣ idem (IX p. 76, col. 2).

ܕܩܘܪܝܐܝܢ Eulogios τῶν χωρικῶν (IX p. 77, col. 1).

ܒܩܘܪܝܢܬܘܣ 2 Cor. **1**. 1. ἐν Κορίνθῳ (VIII p. 134, col. 4). ܠܩܘܪܝܢܬܘܣ 2 Cor. **1**. 23. εἰς Κόρινθον (VIII p. 136, col. 1). ܩܘܪܝܢܬܝܝ 2 Cor. **6**. 11. Κορίνθιοι (VIII p. 140, col. 3).

ܩܛܐ ܡܪܘܣܐ Martyrs κατὰ μέρος sigillatim (IX p. 50, col. 2).

ܩܦܝܐ Acts **27**. 16. τῆς σκάφης (VIII p. 100, col. 1).

ܩܝܢܕܝܢܘܣ Eulogios κινδυνεύω (IX p. 65, col. 2). ܩܝܢܕܝܢܘܣ 1 Cor. **15**. 30. κινδυνεύομεν (VIII p. 130, col. 3).

ܠܩܝܣܪܝܢ Acts **21**. 8. εἰς Καισαρίαν (VIII p. 88, col. 2).

ܠܩܦܣ Gal. **1**. 18. Κηφᾶν (VIII p. 146, col. 3).

ܠܩܦܪܘܣ Acts **21**. 3. τὴν Κύπρον (VIII p. 88, col. 1).

ܩܢܘܡܝ Rom. **15**. 14. αὐτὸς ἐγώ (VIII p. 114, col. 1).

ܩܝܪܘܣ in wax κηρός (VIII p. 200, col. 2).

ܩܪܛ Eulogios κεράτιον (IX p. 61, cols. 1, 2).

ܩܠܘܕܐ Acts **27**. 16. Κλαῦδα (VIII p. 100, col. 1).

ܩܠܘܣܡܐ Martyrs Κλύσμα (IX p. 28, col. 1).

ܩܠܝܐ Martyrs οἴκημα aedicula (IX p. 21, col. 2).

ܩܠܡܘܣ calamus pen (VIII p. 192, col. 4).

ܩܠܟ ܩܠܟܝܢ Job **7**. 5. βώλακας (VIII p. 30, col. 1).

ܩܢܐ ܩܢܐܐ Matt. **27**. 18. φθόνον (VIII p. 60, col. 4). ܘܩܢܝ
Joel **2**. 18. καὶ ἐζήλωσεν (VIII p. 8, col. 1). ܩܢܝ,
Deut. **6**. 15. ζηλωτής (VIII p. 10, col. 2). ܠܩܢܝܢ
Deut. **7**. 6. περιούσιον (VIII p. 14, col. 1).

ܩܢܝܐ Lev. **8**. 26. κανοῦ Pesh. ܣܠܐ (VIII p. 4, col. 3).

ܘܩܢܝ Matt. **27**. 29. καὶ κάλαμον (VIII p. 62, col. 2).

ܩܣܛܪܘܢ Martyrs Castrum κάστρον (IX pp. 31, 48, col. 2).

ܩܪܐ ܢܩܪܐ Martyrs ἐπικαλεσόμεθα (IX p. 33, col. 1).

ܩܪܝܬܐ Eulogios τὸ κτῆμα (IX p. 77, col. 1).

ܩܪܒ ܕܩܪܒܘܬܗܘܢ τῆς στρατείας αὐτῶν of their warfare (VIII p. 190, col. 3).

ܩܪܝܛܐ Acts **27**. 7. τὴν Κρήτην (VIII p. 98, col. 2).

ܠܩܪܝܛܐ Acts **27**. 13. idem (VIII p. 100, col. 1).

ܩܪܥ ܡܬܩܪܥܝܢ 1 Cor. **4**. 11. Arab. قرع Heb. קרע ἀστατοῦμεν (VIII p. 120, col. 3).

ܩܫܛ ܒܩܘܫܛܐ Truly (VIII p. 196, col. 3; p. 198, col. 1).

ܩܫܛܐܝܬ Phil. **2**. 20. γνησίως (VIII p. 162, col. 3).

ܩܫܝ ܩܫܝܐ Acts **25**. 7. βαρέα (VIII p. 90, col. 4); ܒܩܘܫܝܐ Acts **27**. 16. μόλις (VIII p. 100, col. 1).

ܪ

ܪܒ ܪܒܐ Martyrs μεγάλου (IX p. 29, col. 1). ܘܪܒܪܒܢܐ 1 Sam. **6**. 12. καὶ οἱ σατράπαι (VIII p. 24, col. 4).

ܪܒܪܒܢܐ 1 Sam. **6**. 18. σατραπῶν (VIII p. 26, col. 3)

ܪܣܝ ܪܣܝ Heb. **9**. 21. ἐράντισεν (VIII p. 76, col. 1).

ܪܓܙ ܕܪܘܓܙ Eph. **2**. 3. ὀργῆς (VIII p. 156, col. 3).

ܪܓܠ ܪ̈ܓܠܝ Cant. **5**. **3**. τοὺς πόδας μου (VIII p. 194, col. 4).

ܪܗܛ ܪܗܛܘ ܒܬܪ 1 Cor. **14**. 1. Διώκετε (VIII p. 122, col. 4).

ܪܘܚ ܪܘܚܬܐ πνεύματα (VIII p. 198, col. 4).

ܪܚܨ ܪܚܨܝ ܬܘܟܠ Job **6**. 13. ἐπεποίθειν (VIII p. 18, col. 4).

ܪܛܢ ✠ܪ̈ܛܢܝܢ Phil. **2**. 14. γογγυσμῶν cf. Thes. Syr. p. 3895 (VIII p. 162, col. 1).

ܪܝܫ ܪ̈ܝܫܘ 1 Cor. **15**. 24. ἀρχήν (VIII p. 130, col. 1). Eph. **1**. 21. ἀρχῆς (VIII p. 156, col. 1).

ܒܪܝܬܘ ἐν τῇ Ῥαιθοῦ (IX p. 54, col. 1).

ܪܣܡ ܪܣܡܣܐ Mark **2**. 4. τὴν στέγην (VIII p. 72, col. 1).

ܪܟܥ ܡܪܟܥ bow Arab. ركع (VIII p. 194, col. 3).

ܪܩܫ ܐܪܩܫ Gal. **4**. 27. *Imperative.* ῥῆξον (VIII p. 150, col. 4). ܪܩܫܘܢܐ Eph. **5**. 18. ἀσωτία (VIII p. 160, col. 3).

ܪܝܩ ܪ̈ܝܩܢܬܐ Job **6**. 6. κενοῖς (VIII p. 18, col. 2). ܬܬܪܝܩܢ 1 Cor. **1**. 17. κενωθῇ (VIII p. 116, col. 4).

ܪܫܥ ✠ܪ̈ܫܥܝܢ 2 Tim. **3**. 4. προπετεῖς (VIII p. 174, col. 1).

ܫ

ܫܐܠ ܘܫܐܠܬܝ Job **6**. 8. μου ἡ αἴτησις (VIII p. 18, col. 3). ܫܐ̈ܘܠܝܢ Eulogios συναδελφοί beggars (IX p. 55, col. 2). ܕܫܐ̈ܠܢ Acts **25**. 19. ζητήματα (VIII p. 92, col. 4). ܕܫܐܠܬܐ Acts **25**. 26. τῆς ἀνακρίσεως (VIII p. 94, col. 4). ܫܐܠܬܐ 1 Sam. **2**. 20. τοῦ χρέους (VIII p. 20, col. 1). ܕܫܐܠܬ 1 Sam. **2**. 20. οὗ ἔχρησας (VIII p. 20, col. 1). ܫܐܠ ܫܠܡܐ 1 Cor. **16**. 21. Ὁ ἀσπασμός (VIII p. 134, col. 2).

ܫܐܪ ܫܪܝܬ Matt. **25**. 11. *αἱ λοιπαὶ* (VIII p. 54, col. 4).

ܫܒܠ ܘܫܘܒܝܠܝܐ Job **6**. 19. *ἀτραπούς* (VIII p. 28, col. 1). ܫܘ̈ܠܘܝ = ܫܘܒ̈ܠܘܝ Mark **1**. 3. *τὰς τρίβους αὐτοῦ* (VIII p. 68, col. 2).

ܫܐܒܐ Eulogios *κελεύεις* (IX p. 68, col. 2).

ܫܒܥ ܫܘܒܥܐ Lev. **12**. 2. *ἑπτὰ* (VIII p. 6, col. 2).

ܫܒܩ ܫܘܒܘܩܐ Heb. **9**. 22. *ἄφεσις* (VIII p. 76, col. 1).

ܫܒܫ ܒܬܫܒܘܫܐ in haste (VIII p. 192, col. 2). ܒܫܒܫܐܝܬ Martyrs *παραχρῆμα* (IX p. 31, col. 2). ܫܒ̈ܫܝܢ Martyrs ramos *θαλλοῦς* (IX p. 48, col. 1). ܫܘܒ̈ܫܝܢ idem (IX p. 26, col. 2).

ܫܒܬ ܘܫܒܬܐ Matt. **23**. 23. *καὶ τὸ ἄνηθον* (VIII p. 50, col. 3).

ܫܠܠ ܕܫܠܝܠܝܐ 2 Pet. **3**. 17. *τῶν ἀθέσμων* (VIII p. 188, col. 1)

ܫܬܩ ܫܬܝ̈ܩܝܢ Acts **19**. 36. *κατεσταλμένους* (VIII p. 84, col. 3). ܒܫܬܝܩܘܬܐ Martyrs silentio *ἡσυχίως* (IX p. 2, col. 2). ܕܐܫܬܘܩ *ἵνα σιωπήσω* (IX p. 49, col. 2). ܘܒܫܬܝܩܘ idem (IX p. 3, col. 1).

ܫܘܐ ܕܠܐ ܫܘܐܝ Martyrs *τῷ ἀναξίῳ* (IX p. 7, col. 2). ܫܘܐܝ Martyrs *καταξιωθείς* (IX p. 7, col. 2).

ܫܘܒ ܫܘܒܝܢ Eulogios *ἑβδομάδας* (IX p. 71, col. 1). ܫܘܒܐ *ἑβδομάδα* (IX p. 83, col. 1).

ܫܚܐ ܫܚܘܢܐ ܒܬܚܡܡܐ Job **6**. 17. liquefaction, thawing *τακεῖσα θέρμης γενομένης* (VIII p. 28, col. 1).

ܫܝܠܘ 2 Sam. **4**. 3. *Σηλώμ* (VIII p. 22, col. 3).

ܫܝܠ ܫܝܠܝܐ Martyrs flood Arab. سيل (IX p. 35, col. 1).

ܫܝܪ ܫܝܪܐ ܒܫܝܪܬ in the Song of Songs (VIII p. 194, col. 4).

ܫܟܒ ܠܡܫܟܒܘܬܝ Job **7**. 13. *τῇ κοίτῃ μου* (VIII p. 30, col. 3). ܫܠܐܒܝܬܐ = ܫܠܗܒܝܬܐ Martyrs *φλόγα* (IX p. 5, col. 2).

ܫܠܡ ܒܫܠܡ Exod. **4**. 18. *ὑγιαίνων* (VIII p. 2, col. 2). ܕܫܠܡܘܬܐ Lev. **8**. 26. *τῆς τελειώσεως* (VIII p. 4, col. 3). ܕܫܘܠܡܘܬܐ Lev. **8**. 28. idem. ܫܘܠܡ end (VIII p. 192, col. 3). ܫܠܐܡ at peace, released (VIII p. 192, col. 1).

ܫܠܦ ܫܠܦܬ ܐܡܪܬ 2 Cor. **7**. 3. προείρηκα (VIII p. 142, cols. 2, 3).

ܫܡ ܫܐܡ̈ܗܝܢ Eulogios ὀνομάζοντες (IX p. 57, col. 1).

ܫܡܫ ܕܬܫܡܫܘܢ Matt. **6**. 24. δουλεύειν (VIII p. 200, col. 1).

ܫܢܐ ܒܪ ܫܢܝܐ Lev. **12**. 6. ἐνιαύσιον (VIII p. 6, col. 4).

ܫܢܩ ܫܘܢܩܐ 2 Cor. **2**. 4. συνοχῆς (VIII p. 136, col. 2). ܡܫܬܢܩܝܢ 2 Cor. **6**. 12. στενοχωρεῖσθε (VIII p. 140, col 3).

ܫܦ ܠܫܦܝܦܘ 1 Cor. **4**. 3. εἰς ἐλάχιστον (VIII p. 118, col. 3).

ܫܦܝ ܫܘܦܝܐ Rom. **5**. 11. καταλλαγήν (VIII p. 104, col. 3).

ܫܦܪ ܫܐܦܪ Eulogios ἀρέσκει (IX p. 55, col. 2).

ܫܝܢܐ ܫܘܝܢܐ Deut. **7**. 22. καταναλώσει (VIII p. 16, col. 3). ܠܫܝܢܘܗ̄ Job **6**. 9. εἰς τέλος (VIII p. 18, col. 3).

ܫܩܥ ܫܩܥ Acts **20**. 9. καταφερόμενος (submersus est) (VIII p. 86, col. 3).

ܫܩܡ ܠܫܩܡܘܬܐ Ephes. **4**. 19. τῇ ἀσελγείᾳ (VIII p. 158, col. 3).

ܫܪܐ ܠܡܫܪܐ Mark **1**. 7. λῦσαι (VIII p. 68, col. 4). ܘܫܪܝܐܬ Eulogios καὶ ἤρξατο (IX p. 68, col. 2).

ܫܪܩ ܫܪ̈ܩܝܢ ܫܩܪ̈ܝܐ Jer. **12**. 1. οἱ ἀθετοῦντες ἀθετήματα (VIII p. 34, col. 1).

ܫܪܥ ܒܐܫܪܥܘ Gal. **6**. 1. ἐν (τινι) παραπτώματι (VIII p. 154, col. 1). ܕܐܫܪܥܘܬܐ Eph. **4**. 22. τῆς ἀπάτης (VIII p. 158, col. 3). ܫܪܥܬ Eulogios lapsus sum (IX p. 79, col. 2).

ܫܬܐ ܘܢܫܬܐ 1 Cor. **15**. 32. καὶ πίωμεν (VIII p. 130, col. 3). ܐܫܬܐ Matt. **26**. 42. πίω (VIII p. 58, col. 1). ܐܫܬ̈ܘ Matt. **26**. 27. Πίετε (VIII p. 56, col. 2).

ܬ

ܬܓܪ ܠܬܓܘܪܬܢ Eulogios πρὸς τὸ συμφέρον literally τῇ ἐμπορίᾳ ἡμῶν (IX p. 81, col. 2).

ܕܬܗܘܦܢܝܐ Rubric τῆς θεοφανείας (VIII p. 176, col. 2).

ܬܘܒ ܬܐܒܐ Job 7. 7. ἐπανελεύσεται (VIII p. 30, col. 1).

ܬܬܘܒ ܢܦܫܝ Phil. 2. 19. εὐψυχῶ (VIII p. 162, col. 3).

ܕܬܘܠܥܝܐ Job 7. 5. σκωλήκων (VIII p. 30, col. 1).

ܬܪܐ ܬܪܥܝܐ = ܬܪܥܐ Titus 3. 3. νοῦς (VIII p. 176, col. 4). ܕܬܪܥܝܗܘܢ Eph. 4. 17, 23. τοῦ νοὸς αὐτῶν (ὑμῶν) (VIII p. 158, cols. 2, 4).

ܠܬܝܛܪܘܢ Acts 19. 31. εἰς τὸ θέατρον (VIII p. 84, col. 1).

ܬܠܬ ܒܬܠܬܘܬܗܘܢ* 1 Cor. 3. 19. ἐν τῇ πανουργίᾳ αὐτῶν lit. in sua ipsorum triplicatione (VIII p. 118, col. 1). ܒܬܠܬܘ Eph. 4. 14. ἐν πανουργίᾳ (VIII p. 158, col. 1).

ܕܬܝܡܢܝܢ Job 6. 19. Θαιμανῶν (VIII p. 28, col. 1).

ܬܡܗ ܕܬܡܗܗ Eulogios Θαυμάσαι (IX p. 81, col. 2).

ܬܡܡ ♣ܡܬܡܡܝܢ 2 Tim. 3. 3. ἀνήμεροι (VIII p. 174, col. 1).

ܬܡܪ ܐܬܡܘܪܝܢ palm-trees? (VIII p. 198, col. 2).

ܬܢܐ ܬܢܝܢܬܐ Rubric ἡ δευτέρα (VIII p. 144, col. 1).

ܬܩܠ ܕܬܘܩܠܬܐ = ܕܬܘܩܠܐ Rom. 9. 32. τοῦ προσκόμματος (VIII p. 112, col. 1).

ܬܘܦ ܒܬܘܦܝܗ Jer. 12. 5. ἐν φρυάγματι (VIII p. 34, col. 3).

ܬܪܦ ܬܪܦܘ Gal. 6. 8. φθοράν (VIII p. 154, col. 3).

ܬܪܘܪܘܣ Eulogios θυρωρός (IX p. 80, col. 2). ܬܪܘܪܘܣܐ idem (IX p. 72, col. 2).

* This has been verified by Mrs Gibson and by Mr L. Elmslie.

♣ This sign is affixed to some of the words which Dr Hugo Duensing has tried to correct, in the *Deutsche Litteraturzeitung*, 1909, cols. 2398—2400, and in other places, but for which there is sufficient justification both in the MS. and elsewhere. In particular, I cannot see that ܪ̈ܢܢܝܢ in Phil. 2. 14 would be a better translation of γογγυσμοί than ܪ̈ܛܢܝܢ. Those instances in which I accept Dr Duensing's emendations to the text of Cod. Climaci will be found on page 51.

EMENDANDA IN No. VIII

Codex Climaci Rescriptus

The following are those which I accept of Dr Duensing's corrections, to my copy of the MS.

I

Page 88, col. 2, l. 14	*for* ܘܡܚܒܪܢ	*read* ܘܡ̈ܚܒܕܢ
„ 90, col. 3, l. 18	„ ܕܚܒܪ	„ ܕܚܒܕ
„ 92, col. 2, l. 1	„ ܠܝܬܗܘ	„ ܠܝܬ ܗܘ̣
„ 92, col. 4, l. 5	„ ܕܐܬܘܢ	„ ܕܐܬܘ
„ 144, col. 2, l. 5	„ ܫܘܒܗ	„ ܫܘܕܪܐ
„ 175, l. 1	„ ἄσπονδοι, διάβολοι, ἀκρατεῖς, ἀνήμεροι, ἀφιλάγαθοι, 4 προδόται,	„ ἀκρατεῖς, ἀνήμεροι, ἀφιλάγαθοι, ἄσπονδοι, διάβολοι, 4 προδόται,
„ 175, l. 1 of variants, *omit*	3^{1-1} Cod. om. ἄσπονδοι διάβολοι	4^{1} + κατήγοροι
„ 200, col. 4, ll. 14, 15	*for* ܘܠܡ ܐܬܐ ܠܐ ܢܬܡܛܠܐ	*read* ܘܥܡ ܐܬܐ ܠܐ ܢܬܡܠܟܐ
„ 201, l. 19	„ "and for whatsoever cometh, let him not linger."	„ "and let him not converse with a woman."

II

To the MS. itself, which is as I published it.

Page 10, col. 4, l. 21	*for* ܘܐܦܩܝܬܘܢ	*read* ܘܐܦܩ ܬܘܢ
„ 86, col. 3, l. 18	„ ܘܠܦܝܬܗ	„ ܘܠܦ ܬܗ
„ 128, col. 2, l. 19	„ ܡܒܠܬܗ	„ ܡܒܠ ܬܗ
„ 172, col. 1, ll. 11, 12	„ ܘܡܒܣܐ ܕܠܐ ܬܪܦ *sic*	„ ܘܡܒܝܢܐ ܕܠܐ ܬܪܦ

On page 174, col. 1, l. 12 ܕܘ̈ܫܒܝܢ ought not to be ܡܘ̈ܫܒܝܢ, as Dr Duensing has suggested. The first letter is decidedly either a ܕ or a ܪ, when tried with the re-agent. ܘܫ and ܝܢ are certainly right. The fourth letter has not the distinctive marks of either a *nun* or an *'ain*; and as the word required must be an equivalent of προπετεῖς, I have adopted ܪܘ̈ܫܒܝܢ, seeing that its root ܪܫܒ suggests the idea of daring[1]. [Cf. the Hebrew and Chaldee Lexicon of Dr Samuel Davidson, p. 1320.]

This, and the four words in List II, have been verified on the MS. by Mrs Gibson and Mr L. Elmslie.

ܒܣܒܝܪ for ܫܣܒܝܪ p. 152, is not included, as it was one of the six errata acknowledged before publication. It is a mistake of the MS.

[1] Dr Nestle suggested this quite independently of me.

TRANSLATION

f. 32^{b} And the man is mistaken who attributes it to the body, and does[1] not comprehend the interior of the matter. The Christ is in every place; no place can contain Him. And also the Book has described the Christ, that He is in every place, and no place is empty of Him; and no place contains Him. The Gospel says that
John 14. the Christ said, "Whoso loveth Me, he will keep My commandments, and My
23 Father will love him, and We will come and will make our abode with him." And
Matt. 18. He said in another place, "that where two or three are gathered together in My
20 name, I shall be there amongst them." I think that He is not in an empty place, He who can be in every place; and if the Christ were only the flesh, which He took from Mary, He would not describe that; He is not contained in that. And the Book describes the Christ; but He describes Himself, that He is amongst all those who are gathered together because of His name. And it is known that *people* are assembled in His name every morning and in every hidden place, and at every hour in the day and the night; and specially amongst sinners and slaves, all the people at the ends of the earth, and in the most distant places of it. And He is amongst them as He said. And He is also amongst those who do His commandments, according as He said. And if some of them are separated from the others from one end of it to the other, His Father also is with him, and the power of both. And the Christ is not even that body which appeared; but He is the very Son of God, Who is with His Son in every place. And no place is empty of Him, just like His Father. And because of this He is God like Him. And he is mistaken who doubts because a body is kept entire or is cut to pieces, this *being* His dwelling and the dwelling of His Father which stretches out from His dwelling unto life everlasting. (*erasure*) And also the Book relates about the Christ, that He knows
John 2. all the secrets of men. The Gospel says that the Christ, "when He was in
23—25 Jerusalem at the feast of the Passover, many believed in Him, because they saw the miracles which He did; and Jesus did not trust them, and did not confide in them in regard to Himself, because He knew all men; and did not need that any should testify to Him about any man, for He knew all that was within all men." I think that He did not know the fault of all men because of this, that he (man) is created. And if the Christ had been only this created flesh, which He put on from Mary, He would not have been described in that way.

And the Book describes the Christ, that He knew that. The Christ said: "This flesh that appears has been born of (*erasure*) the interior, who knoweth all the secrets like God; and because of that, (*erasure*) whoever doubts about it is mistaken, and is not at peace with him, and he does not trust to himself...

[1] Arab. "do."

A PAGE OF THE ARABIC UPPER SCRIPT

(f. 32b) وقد ضل الذى ينسبوه الى الجسد ولم يعقلوا باطن امره ⁘ المسيح[1]
فى كل مكان لا يحوى عليه مكان ، وايضا قد وصف الكتاب المسيح انه فى
كل مكان ولم يخلوا منه مكان ولا يحتوى عليه موضع ، قال الانجيل[2] ان
المسيح قال ان من يحبنى وصياى هو[3] يحفظ وابى يحبه ونحن ناتيه ونصير John 14. 23
عنده المسكن ، وقال فى موضع اخر انه اذا اجتمع ائنين او ثلثة على اسمي Matt. 18. 20
فانا ثم بينهم ، اظن انه ليس فى المخلو فين من يستطيع يكون فى كل
مكان ولو ان المسيح ليس الا البشسر الذى اخذ من مريم قد لم يوصف لذلك
لا بذلك محتوى ، وقد وصف الكتاب المسيح بل هو[3] وصف نفسه انه بين
كل من يجتمع من اجل اسمه ومعروف انه يجتمع من اجل اسمه فى كل
غداة وغشية وساعات النهار ولياليها وخاصه فى الخاطاين[4] والعباد جميع الناس
فى اقاصي الارض[5] واباعدها وهو[6] بينهم كما قال ، وايضا هو[3] بين من عمل
وصياه على ما قال وان بعد بعضهم عن بعض من طرف الى طرفها وابوه
معه وسلطنهم ، فليس المسيح هذا الجسد الذى ظهر قط ولكنه بن الله الباطن
الذى هو[3] مع ابنه فى كل مكان ولا يخلوا منه مكان مثل ابيه ، ومن اجل ذلك
فهو[7] الله مثله ، وقد ضل الذى يشك من اجل انه اشتمل جسد او فاتته سكانه
وسكانه ابيه التى يمد من سكناه الحياة الدايمه ⁘ erasure وايضا قد
وصف الكتاب المسيح انه يعرف جميع سراير الناس ، قال الانجيل[2] ان المسيح
حيث كان فى اوروسلم فى عيد الفصح كثيرا امنوا به لانهم راوا عاجيبه
التى كان يعمل ولم يكن يسوع يضمن[8] اليهم ولا يتامنهم[9] على نفسه ، لانه قد John 2. 23—25
كان يعرف جميع الناس ولم يكن يحتاج يسهد عنده على احد من الناس
لانه قد كان يعلم باطن جميع الناس اظن لا يعلم عيب جميع الناس من
اجل ذلك مخلوق ولو ان المسيع لم يكن الا هذا البشر المخلوق الذى اكتساه
من مريم قد لم يوصف بذلك وقد وصف الكتاب المسيح انه قد كان يعلم
ذلك فال مسيح ليس هذا البشر الظاهر قد ولد من erasure الباطن الذى
يعرف جميع السرابر مثل ابيه ومن اجل ذلك erasure قد ضل من شك فيه
ولا يطمان الله اليه ولا يستند على نفسه

---

[1] Cod. المسميح [2] Cod. النجيل [3] Cod. هوا [4] Cod. الحطاين
[5] Cod. الرض [6] Cod. وهوا [7] Cod. فهوا [8] Cod. يضمان [9] Cod. يتمنهم

f. 49 b ܫܘܒܚܐ ܀
ܘܕܝܗܐ
ܡܫܒܚܝܢ ܠܗ
ܡܢ ܕܬܪܒܐ
ܘܡܟܢܫ ܘܐܙܠ
ܠܗ ܕܠܐ
ܡܡܠܠ ܒܦܡܗ ܀
ܐܠܐ ܕܝ
ܝ... ܬ ܢܫܦ
⌜ܚ⌝ܒ ܦܡܗ̇
ܕܡܒܪܬܐ
ܒܬܝܒ: ܐܬܝ
f. 56 a ܢܬܗ: ܘܗܒܝܢ
ܗܘܐ ܐܚܘܢ
ܒܒܝ ܡܠܐ
ܠܗ ܚܕ ܓܒܪ
ܕܩܝܡ ܒܒܘܠ
ܫܘܒܚܐ ܀ ܘܗܘܐ
ܡܒܐ ܒܬܒ
ܒܢܫܦܐ ܡܢܐ
ܕܗܘ ܓܪܝܢ
ܘܗܘܐ ܐܚܘܢ

f. 49 b ܡܫܒܚܝܢ
ܓܒܪܐ ܕܡܢܝܐ
ܗܘ ܕܦܩܕܗ̇
ܕܡܒܪܬܐ ܀
ܘܢܫܒ
ܢܫܦܐ
ܕܒܬܝܒ ܀
ܘܡܟܢܫ ܘܐܙܠ
ܠܗ ܘܠܐ
ܡܡܠܠ ܒܦܡܗ
ܗܝܢ ܦܘܩܕܗ
ܕܫܒܩܐ ܀ ܘܗܘܐ
f. 56a ܡܪܝ ܕܢܝܐܝܠ
ܩܪܐ ܒܟܬܒܐ
ܕܫܒܩܐ
ܘܝܗܒ ܠܗ
ܓܘܪܒܗ ܀
ܒܚܕ ܕܝ ܡܢ
ܝܘܡܝܐ ܐܫܟܚ
ܢܫܦܐ[1] ܒܬܝܒ
ܗܒܕܢ: ܐܬܝܬܐ
ܡܢ ܚܕܐ ܐܬܬ

[1] Arab. صحيفة

f. 49 a ܕ̈ܢܫܡܥܘܢ
ܘܥܕܡ ܒܢܝܢܐ
ܕܢܫܠܛܐ
ܒܪ̈ܒܘܬܗ:
ܕܢܫܠܘ̈ܬܗܘܢ
ܕܟܘܠ
ܦܪ̈ܨܘܦܐ
ܐܡܝܢ

ܗܢܐ ܕܛܘܢ ܐܒܐ
ܕܢܝܐܝܠ ܠܬܠܡܝܕܗ
f. 56 b ܥܠ ܦܓܪܗ ܕܦܛܪܝܩܝܐ ܀
ܐܒܐ ܕܢܝܐܝܠ
ܬܘܒ ܥܠ ܦܓܪ
ܚܕ ܣܪ̇ܝܣ
ܕܗܘܐ
ܒܡܕܒܪܐ
ܓܘܝܐ
ܕܐܣܩܝܛܝܣ ܀

f. 49 a ܘܗܘܬ
ܡܠܟܬܗ
ܪ̇ܘܡܐ ܗܘܝܢ
ܬܘܫܒܚܬܐ ܒܥܕܪ̈
ܡܫ̈ܠܡܝܢ ܗܘ
ܐܣܩܝܛܝܣ ܀
ܘܫܪܐ ܗܘ
ܗܘܐ ܐܬܐ
ܠܘܬ ܐܒܐ
ܕܢܝܐܝܠ
ܒܫܘܒܬܐ
ܒ[ ]ܠܠܝܐ
f. 56 b ܘܠܐ ܗܘܐ
ܐܢܫ ܚܕ
ܒܗ ܐܠܐ
ܬܠܡܝܕܗ
ܒܠܚܘܕ ܀
ܘܒܬܪ ܫܒܥܐ
ܠܬܠܡܝܕܗ
ܕܗܘܐ ܡܠܟܐ
ܠܗ ܚܕ ܙܒܢ
ܕܚ̈ܫܝܢ ܒܟܘܠ

f. 6b ܟܘܠ ܗ̈ܢ
ܦܪܘܫܐ
ܐܠܗܐ ܐܝܟ
ܠܗ ܘܡܫܝܚܠ
ܠܗ: ܘܡܚܒܠ
ܒܟܘܠ ܝܘܡ
ܫܪ̈ ܦܪܓܠ ⁖
ܗܐ ܐܘܢ
ܐܡܪܬܝ ܠܝ
ܡܢ ܗܢ ܐܢܐ
ܡܒܪ ܠܗ ⁖
f. 3a ܘܬܡܗ ܕܝ
ܬܠܡܝܕܗ
ܕܫܒܐ ܟܠ
ܟܘܠ ܡܒܐ
ܕܫܘܒܪ
ܫܒܐ ܡܢ
ܠܒܝܬ
ܝܪܒܘܬܗ
ܕܐܘܠܘܓܝܣ ⁖
ܗܠܝܢ ܓܠܐ
ܐܝܟܐ ܕܢܐܙܠ

f. 6b ܠܬܠܡܝ̈ܕܗ
ܡܢ ܒܬܪ
ܕܬܒ ܡܢ
ܬܝܒܐܝܫ ⁖
ܢܦܠ ܠܝ ܕܝ
ܕܢܬܒܢܗ
ܥܠ ܪ̈ܓܠܘܗܝ
ܕܐܠܗܐ ⁖
ܕܗܒܢ
ܠܝܡܝܢܐ
ܦܪܘܫܗ
f. 3a ܪ̈ܘܚܢ
ܘܡܟܝܢ:
ܗܝܢ ܕܝ
ܠܬܠܡܝܕܬܐ
ܕܝܠܝ ⁖ ܢܦܠ ܕܝ
ܕܐܘܦ ܐܝܢ
ܢܬܡܟܝܢ
ܒܝܬܗ
ܕܡܢܝܢ ܫܘܫܘ
ܡܫܝܚܐ ⁖ ܗܝܢ
ܕܢܩܒܠ

f. 6a ○ܐܡܪ ܠܗ
ܓܠ ܒܠܐܝ
ܡܪܝ ܕܐܒܐ
ܡܫܡܫܝܢ
ܘܠܝܬ ܒܝܢ
ܐܚܝ ܚܠܘܦ܃
○ܐܒܐ ܐܡܪܬ
ܠܗ ܐܘܠܦܢ
ܕܝ ܡܟܐ
ܕܗܘܐ ܠܟ
ܠܐ ܗܘܐ ܠܟ܃
ܘܐܡܪ ܠܗ
f. 3b ܠܒܢܐ ܡܪܝ
ܐܢܫ ܒܚܠܘܦ
ܐܒܫܠܝܬ ܠܘܬܟ܃
ܘܐܡܪܬ ܠܗ
ܒܡܟܐ ܓܪ ܠܐ
ܒܫܠܝܬ ܠܘܬܝ܃
ܘܒܗ ܐܡܪܬ
ܠܗ ܒܥܘܠܐ
ܘܐܘܦ ܟܠ
ܡܫܘܚܬܐ

f. 6a ܗܠܝܢ ܕܠܒܘܬ
ܡܢ ܬܪܘܪܗ܃
ܘܒܒܝܢ
ܗܝܟ ܫܒܐ܃
ܘܐܡܪ ܠܗ
ܓܠ ܕܫܓܪ
ܠܐ ܐܠܗܐ
ܒܪܚܬܐ܃
ܘܡܢ ܒܕܘ ܐܒܐ
ܡܫܘܝ ܠܒܪܗ܃
ܘܐܡܪܬ ܠܗ
ܗܝܡܢ ܠܝ
f. 3b ܡܪܝ ܐܘܠܦܢ
ܕܡܢ ܒܕܘ ܠܐ
ܬܫܒܚܐ ܕܐܒܐ
ܡܬܗܝܡܢ
ܒܚܠܘܦ ܡܢ
ܗܕܐ ܒܕܢ
ܠܡܟܐ ܐܠܐ
ܡܢ ܫܕ ܦܫܪܘ
ܒܘܠ ܝܘܩ܃
ܘܗܘܐ ܐܘܢ

f. 57 b ܘܟܕ ܕܝ
⸢ܫ⸣ܡܥܐ ܗܘܝ
ܒܪܡܫܐ ܀
⸢ܐ⸣ܬܐ ܘܕܒܪ
ܗܘܝ ܗܢܘܢ
*ܩܫܝ⸢ܫ⸣ܬܐ
ܕܠܗ ܀
⸢ܘ⸣ܟܕ ܕܝ
⸢ܫ⸣ܡܥܬ ܗܘܬܗ
ܐܬܬܢܚܬ
ܘܒܟܬ
ܘܐܡܪܬ ܀
f. 64 a ܡܢܐ ܕܒ̈ܢܝܢ
ܠܘܒܕܢܝ
ܡܢܐ ܠܘܠܐ
ܒܠܥܐ
ܠܒܪܬ ܀
ܡܡܥܡܢܝ
ܘܡܪܘܡܡ ܀
ܠܒ̈ܢܝܢ
ܘܠܒܢ̈ܬܝܢ
ܡܢ ܟܠ

f. 57 b ܕܡܣܒܒ
ܡܪܐ
ܐܠܗܐ ܀
ܐܢܐ ܕܝ
ܐܣܬܠܩܬ
ܒܡܟܐ ܕܐܬܚܝܬ
ܥܪܐ ܢܦܫܝ
ܐܫܬܪܪܬ
ܒܫܘܠ ܢܦܫܝ ܀
ܘܢܦܫ ܡ̈ܢܝ
ܘܐܫܟܚ ܪ̈ܓܠܝ
ܗܢܘܢ ܐܦ
f. 64 a ܩܫܝܫܬܐ
ܕܠܗ ܀
ܘܐܬܬܡ
ܦܬܘܪܐ ܀
ܘܡܢ ܒܬܪ
ܕܝ ܕܐܟܠܘ
ܐܡܪܬ
ܠܗ ܡܢܐ ܐܬ
ܒܥܝܐ ܐܢܬܝ
ܐܘܠܘܓ ܀

* Cod. ܩܫܝܬܐ

f. 57a ܩܘܡ ܒܡܚܘܠ
ܐܘܠܨ ܀
ܗܒܐ ܠܝ
ܗܝ ܡܟܝܪܢ ܀
ܘܗܒ ܠܝ ܢܝܒ
ܢܝܒ ܐܬܐ
ܠܡܫܝܚܘܬܐ
ܕܠܗ
ܡܟܝܢܬܐ
ܒܡܫܝܚܗ
ܕܡܪܝ ܫܘܦܘ ܀
ܠܝܬ ܠܝ
f. 64b ܐܠܗܐ
ܦܐܠܘܨ ܀
ܕܡܬܒܥܐ
ܒܥܒܕܘܗܝ
ܡܟܝܢ ܗܠܝܢ
ܕܒܒܪ ܀ ܘܗܟܢ
ܒܬܪ ܢܝܫܐ
ܡܢܪܘܫ
ܫܠܡܬ
ܠܗ ܡܪܬܐ ܀

f. 57a ܡܬܪܓܡ ܀
ܘܢܩܒ
ܒܘܪܙܠܐ
ܘܢܦܩ
ܠܡܟܝܪܐ
ܠܗ ܕܐܒܥܝ
ܕܗܒܐ ܀
ܣܒܝܪ ܕܗܘ
ܡܟܒܫ ܕܗܒ
ܚܘܪ ܠܗ ܬܚܙܡ ܀
ܘܐܡܪ ܗܢܝ
ܫܒܬ ܥܒܕܝܢ ܀
f. 64b ܘܠܐ ܐܫܟܚ
ܟܠܘܡ ܀ ܘܫܪܝ
ܡܬܕܟܪ
ܒܡܚܫܒܬܐ
ܗܠܝܢ ܀
ܘܠܐܝܢܐ ܗܘ ܀
ܘܠܬܫܒܘܚܬܐ
ܕܓܒܘܬܐ
ܕܗܘܐ ܒܗܝܢ ܀
ܘܐܡܪ

f. 40b ܡܩܪܝܐ
ܗܘܬ ܡܗܘܬ ܀
ܘܚܙܘ ܘܐܬܐ
ܠܗ ܠܡܪܬܗ
ܘܫܠܛ
ܡܐܢ̈ܘܗܝ ܗܘܝܢ
ܕܦܘܪ̈ܐܝܢ ܀
ܘܐܬܒܢܝܬ
ܒܟܠܗ
ܩܪܝܬܐ ܟܠܗ̇
ܕܫܡܥܘܢ ܡܛܠܗ ܀
ܘܐܡܪ̈ܝܢ
f. 33a ܕܫܡܥܢܢ ܕܐܬܐ
ܦܛܪܝܩܝܘܣ
ܐܬܚܒܕܬ ܀
ܘܐܡܪ ܠܗܘܢ
ܐܝܢ ܀ ܐܠܘ ܗܘ
ܐܬܚܒܕܬ
ܦܛܪܝܩܝܘܣ
ܗܘܐ ܠܐ
ܕܫܡܥܐ
ܡܛܠܘܢ ܀

f. 40b ܠܟ. ܐܠܐ
ܚܘܪܢ ܗܘܐ
ܐܘܠܘܓܝܣ
ܡܢ ܗܕܢ
ܐܬܪܐ ܀
ܐܢܐ ܓܒܪ
ܒܪܘܫܠܝܡ
ܗܘܝܬ ܡܩܠܐ ܀
○ܒܝܢ ܐܬܐ
ܠܗܘܢܗ
ܘܗܘܐ
ܐܡܪ
f. 33a ܠܦܪܥܗ: ܐܘ
ܡܣܟܢܐ
ܗܘܠܘܓܝ ܀
ܡܘܕ ܗܢ
ܦܘܪܠܝܢ
ܘܐܙܠ ܒܡܘܠ ܀
ܕܒܐ ܠܝܬ
ܥܠܠܝܢ ܠܐ
ܐܘܢ ܐܘܦ.
ܪܫܝܢ

f. 40a ܐܬܒܪܟܬ
ܒܫܪܘܐ ܪܒܐ ܀
ܕܐܬܦܩܕܬ
ܡܢ ܡܪܒܘܬܗ
ܕܐܘܠܘܓܝܣ ܀
ܘܦܪܫܬ ܐܘܢ
ܒܝܕܥܐ ܕܗܘܐ
ܠܐܠܗܐ ܀
ܘܡܢ ܒܬܪ
ܕܝ ܬܠܬܐ
ܫ̈ܢܝܢ ܡܢܬ
ܝܘܣܛܝܢܘܣ
f. 33b ܡܠܟܐ ܀ ܘܡܠܟ
ܝܘܣܛܝܢܝܢܘܣ ܀
ܘܡܕ̈ܪܘ
ܠܗܘܢ
ܗܦܝܛܘܣ
ܘܐܣܦܩܘܪܛܘܣ
ܘܩܘܡܒܝܢܘܣ
ܘܐܘܠܘܓܝܣ
ܐܦܪܟܐ ܀
ܘܗܠܝܢ ܕܝ

f. 40a ܬܠܝܬܝܐ
ܐܬܦܬܠܠ
ܘܐܬܒܢܝ
ܒܘܠܗ
ܒܘܬܪܗܘܢ ܀
ܘܐܘܦ
ܐܘܣܝܐ
ܕܐܘܠܘܓܝܣ
ܘܒܘܠ
ܒܘܬܪܐ
ܕܠܗ ܀ ܘܒܪܘܡ
ܒܠܠܝܐ
f. 33b ܒܠܝܘܕ
ܒܡܐܢ̈ܝܐ
ܕܗܘܘ ܒܠ
ܦܘܓܪܗ ܀
ܘܢܦܐܘ ܡܢ
ܘܣܛܝܢܝܢܘܒܘܠܣ ܀
ܘܒܘܡ ܡܠܟܐ
ܕܒܘܠ ܗܘ
ܕܫܬܒܫ
ܐܘܠܘܓܝܣ

f. 77b ܠܥܒܕܠ ܒܪܘܟܬܗ
ܕܐܘܠܘܓܝܣ
ܐܢܐ ܓܠܝܐ ܀
ܘܐܡܪܬ
ܠܝ ܐܢܐ
ܡܦܝܣܐ
ܚܠܦܝܢ: ܘܡܣܟܢܬ
ܡܬܗ̇ ܕܐܝܠܬ
ܘܢܩܒܬ
ܕ̈ܟܠܘܝ
ܕܗ̇ܘ ܓܠܝܐ ܀
f. 78a ܘܒܗ̇ ܒܢܟܬܐ
ܐܚܬܘ ܠܝ̇
ܕܗܘܝܬ ܬ̇ܠܐ ܀
ܘܐܡܪ ܠܝ
ܗܘ ܓܠܝܐ
ܠܐ ܡܢ ܒܕܘ
ܬܚܒܒܕ
ܡܡܫܬܐ
ܗܕܐ ܀ ܐܢܐ
⌜ܐܡܪ⌝ܬ

f. 77b ܠܐ ܡܢܝ ܀
ܠܥܒܕܠ
ܗܕܐ ܓܝܪ
ܐܦܝܣܬ
ܡܢܝ ܗܘܝܢ
ܕܡܬܢܪܐܬ
ܡܥܪܝ ܀
ܐܣܬܠܩܬ ܀
ܢܒܘܫ ܠܝ ܀
ܘܦܓܪ ܘܪܥܘ
ܡܬܝ ܀ ܘܐܡܪ
f. 78a ܠܝ. ܐܙܠ ܠܟ
ܠܡܕܝܢܬܟ ܘܐܢܐ
ܡܬܚܬܐ ܠܗ
ܠܐܘܠܘܓܝܣ
ܠܥܒܕܬܗ
ܡܫܚܬܐ
ܘܠܐ ܬܟܣܐ ܀
ܪܥܝ ܡܠܟܘܢ ܀
ܘܟܕ ܐܘܢ
ܐܬܒܝܪܬ

f. 77a ܒܥܠܡܗ
ܦܓܪ̈ܝ
ܐܬܬܪ ܀
ܘܠܐ ܢܓܠܝܬ
ܕܢܦܬܘܚ
ܦܘܡܝ ܘܢܒܥ
ܠܒܝ ܒܓܘܗ ܀
ܘܐܡܪ ܠܝ
ܗܘ ܗܘ
ܒܪܘܫܬܟ ܀
ܘܐܡܪ ܠܬܠܬܝܢ
f. 78b ܡܢ ܗܠܝܢ
ܕܡܫ̈ܡܫܝܢ
ܘܩܪܒܘܢܝ
ܕܢܦܩܘܢܬܘܢ
ܠܝ ܘܬܠܘܢ
ܠܝ ܘܦ̈ܬܓܡܝ
ܒܦܘ̈ܡܟܘܢ
ܠܡܪܝܐ ܀
ܘܐܡܪ ܠܝ
ܠܐ ܬܒ̈ܥܘܢ
ܒܐܝܕ ܕܠܝܬ

f. 77a ܡܢܝܢ ܀ ⌜ܘܐ⌝ܬܬ
⌜ܬܠ⌝ܝܬܝܐ
ܡܢ ܐܠܗܐ ܀
ܘܠܐ ܗܘܝܬ
ܢܟܠ ܦܬܝܟ
ܦܡܟ ܀ ܘܗܘܝܢ
ܕܐܢܐ ܬܠܐ ܀
ܐܬܐ ܘܠ
ܐܡܪ ܗܐ
ܡܠܟܘܬܐ
ܢܦܘܩ ܀ ܘܢܒܥ
ܫܡܝܢ ܬܗ̈ܘ
f. 78b ܐܬܠܒܒܢܬ ܀
ܘܐܡܪܢ ܠܗ
ܒܟܠ ܡܢܝܢ ܀
ܐܬܪܫܡ
ܥܠ ܡܬܪܬܗ
ܕܥܠܡܐ ܀
ܘܐܡܪܬ
ܠܗ ܟܡܐ
ܐܬ ܒܒܐ
⌜ܘܐܡܪܢ ܠ⌝ܗ

f. 21b ܡܢ ܡܫ̈ܡܫܘܬܐ
ܘܡܢ ܡܢܐ
ܕܗܘܘ
ܡܙܒܢܝܢ
ܒܗ܀ ܘܒܢܝܢ
ܐܡܪܝܬ
ܐܙܠ ܐܢܫܐ ܠܟ
ܠܐܣܩܝܬܝܣ܀
ܘܐܝܟ ܒܥܐ
ܐܠܗܐ ܦܩܕ
ܗܘ ܠܟ ܘܐܘܦ
ܠܐܘܠܘܓܝܣ܀
f. 16a ܘܡܢ ܐܙܠܝܬ
ܘܒܥܝܬ ܐܠܗ̇
ܐܠܨܬܢܝ
ܕܢܐܙܠ ܠܟ
ܠܐܬܪܝ܀
ܘܐܫܟܚܬ
ܐܠܗ ܘܣܠܩܬ
ܠܗ ܗܟܢ
ܕܢܐܬܐ ܠܟ
ܠܘܬܟ܀

f. 21b ܘܒܙ ܕܝ
ܣܠܩܝܬ
ܠܐܠܦܐ
ܘܡܢ ܕܒܘܪܬ
ܢܦܩ ܢܐܡܢܝܬ܀
ܘܗܝܟܢ ܕܐܢܐ
ܕܡܟܝܢ ܫܡܥܬ
ܕܝ ܗܝܟܢ
ܕܗܘܝܬ
ܒܡܕܝܢܬܝ
ܩܢܐܡܬܐ
ܡܕܝܢܬܐ܀
f. 16a ܘܫܡܥܬ
ܠܗܘ ܓܒܠܝܐ
ܕܬܒ ܥܠ
ܟܦܐ ܡܘܕܥ
ܒܡܕܝܢܬܐ
ܡܕܝܢܬܐ:
ܘܐܕܒܪ
ܒܝ ܒܝܠܦܐ
ܟܒܐ ܕܡܢ
ܕܥܠܬܗ

f. 21a ܐܠܗܝܢ
ܘܪ̈ܘܒܐܢ
ܕܥܠܡܝܢ ܆
ܘܦܪܝܬ
ܘܐܡܪܝܬ
ܡܪܬܝ
ܐܬܪܚܡܝ
ܥܠܝ ܆ ܘܐܡܪܬ
ܠܝ ܡܢܐ ܠܟܝ
ܘܐܡܪܝܬ ܠܗ̇
ܕܐܘܠܨܢܝ
ܐܦܪܢܐ
f. 16b ܒܪܢܒܬ ܆
ܐܠܐ ܦܩܘܕܝ
ܕܢܦܫܘܪ ܡܢ
ܒܪܢܒܬܗ ܆
ܘܐܡܪܬ
ܐܢܐ ܠܗ̇
⌈ܢܚܠ⌉
ܗܝܟ ܕܐܬ
ܒܗܝ ⌈ܡܚܠ⌉
ܒܪܢܒܬܟܝ ܆

f. 21a ܘܐܬܒܢܝܬ
ܕܝ ܘܒܟܢ
ܐܡܪܝܬ
ܕ⌈ܐܢܐ⌉ ܐܠ⌈ܘ⌉
⌈ܗܘܐ⌉ ⌈ܠܝ⌉
ܕܢܫܘܬ
ܐܢܐ ⌈ܠܐ⌉ ܢܪܝܫܒ
ܡܢ ܬܪܥܗ
ܐܠܐ ܡܠܠܬ
ܒܡܫܗ̇ ܆ ܘܐ⌈ܙ⌉ܠܬ
ܘܝܬܒܬ ܠܗ
ܗܢ ܕܬܪܥܗ̇
f. 16b ܕܒܝܬܗ ܆
ܘܒܪ ܒܒܪ
⌈ܦ⌉ܪܢܒܬ ܘܪܗܛ
ܕܝ ܒܠܐܝ
ܬܪܘܪܦܐ
ܘܝܗܒ ܠܝ
ܡܫܘܐܢ ܒܕ
ܡܢܐ ܕܘܦܕ
ܡܦܕܝ ܆ ܒܟܢ
ܐܒܪܬ ܢܦܫܝ

ܠܗܘܢ ܟܘܠ f. 51b
ܣܘܪܢ ܘܗܘܘ
ܡܚܣܢܝܢ ܠܗ̇ܝ :
ܘܡܒܙܚܝܬ
ܐܪܟܒ ܫܘܒܩܝܢ
ܘܠܐ ܡܠܝܬ
ܕܡܣܪܒ ܒܚܟܡܗ :
ܗܫܪܢ ܟܕ
ܢܦܩ ܘܐܙܠ
ܢܚܪܬ ܠܗܝ
ܩܘܪܒ
ܐܦܝܣܩܘܦܐ f. 54a
ܕܡܕܝܢܬܗ
ܡܪܝܢ
ܒܒܘܚܢܐ :
ܘܗܘܝܬ
ܐܡܪ ܡܪܝ
ܦܘܣ
ܡܫܝܚܐ
ܒܪܗ]
[ܕܐܠܗܐ
ܐܬܪܥܡ

ܟܠܗ̇ ܘܫܪܝ f. 51b
ܠܗܝ ܡܢ
ܒܪܘܟܬܗ
ܕܗܕܐ ܟܒܪܐ :
ܘܐܦ ܕܠܐ
ܐܘܦ ܐܢܐ
ܐܙܠ ܠܟܠܡܐ :
ܘܟܕ ܗܘܐ
ܗܠܝܢ * *
ܕܐܢܐ ܫܡܥܬ
ܘܡܫܝܬ
ܒܒܢ̈ܝܐ, f. 54a
ܡܪܚܝܬ
ܠܗܘܠܐ
ܘܫܡܫܝܬ
ܬܘܡܢ ܡܠ
ܐܟܠܘܗ
ܗܟܢ ܐܡܪ̈ܝܢ
ܕܗܐ ܡܟܠܬܐ
ܕܟܠܡܐ :
ܘܗܘܘ ܐܙܠܝܢ
ܘܡܕܡܝܢ̇

f. 51a ܕܘܝܡܒܢ
ܦܛܪ̈ܝܩܝܘܣ
ܘܟܕ ܕܝ
ܫܡܫܬ
ܕܗܘ ܒܒܢܝ
ܦܛܪܝܩܝܘܣ
ܐܡܪܝܬ
ܒܢܦܫ
ܕܐܢܐ ܗܘ
ܕܒܒܢܝܬ
ܗܕܢ ܦܠܐ ܀
f. 54b ܘܪܡܝܬ
ܗܘ ܟܒܪܐ
ܒ̈ܐܠܦܐ ܘܒܟܡ
ܫܠܡܝܬ
ܠܘܣܛܠܛܦܘܠܝܣ
ܘܗܘܝܬ
ܥܐܠ ܗܢ
ܗܘ ܒܝܬܗ
ܕܡܢܝܪܐ
ܘܐܘܕܥܘ ܠܝ ܀
ܘܬ̈ܒܝܬ

f. 51a ܗܢ ܕܬܪܥܐ
ܕܒܝܬܗ ܀
ܟܕ ܗܘܐ
ܕܗܘ ܢܐܦܩ ܀
ܘܫܡܫܬ
ܠܬܗ ܕܢܩܦ
ܒܦܛܪܝܩܝܘܣ
ܣܠܩ ܀ ܘܩܪܝܬ
ܘܐܡܪܝܬ
ܐܬܪܘܡܣ
ܥܠ ܘܫܡܫܒ
f. 54b ܡܟܢ ܡܐ
ܕܐܢܐ ܒܟܐ
ܕܢܐܡܘܪ
ܠܝ ܀ ܘܠܐ ܐܘܢ
ܐܕܡܝ ܕܝ
ܐܠܐ ܐܘܦ
ܗܠܝܢ ܕܗܘ̈ܘ
ܐܝܠܝܢ ܡܘܕܡܝܢ
ܗ̈ܘܘ ܡܣܝܝܢ
ܠܬܝ ܀ ܘܬܘܒܢ
ܐܡܪ̈ܬ ܗܟܢ

f. 32b ܐܬܬܝܬ ܕܢܣܒܢ
ܒܒܝܪܬܐ
ܕܐܢ̈ܫܝ ܀
ܘܐܡܪܬ ܠܝ
ܐܘܦ ܐܢ
ܡܢܟܢ ܐܢܬ
ܒܒܝܪܬܟ ܠܐ
ܬܫܘܪ
ܒܡܪܬܐ ܀
ܐܠܐ ܐܢ
ܒܟ̈ܒܐ ܐܢܬ
ܕܬܬܡܗ̈ܐ
f. 25a ܡܫܢܝܢܐܝ
ܐܘܠ ܠܟ
ܠܐܦܣܩܘܬܗ ܀

ܪܝܫ ܡܟܠܝܘܢ
ܐܢܐ ܕܝ
ܐܡܪܬ
ܠܟ݁ : ܒܗܝܟܢ
ܣܪܘܟ ܡܢ
ܗܠܝܢ ܥܒ̈ܕܬܐ ܀

f. 32b ܗܘܠܘܦ ܠܝܬ
ܒܗܕܐ ܡܪܬܐ
ܒܪܢܫ ܕܕܝܠ
ܡܢ ܐܠܗܐ
ܕܡܟܠܢܫ
ܐܟܫܢܐܝܢ ܀
ܘܐܡܪܬ ܠܝ
ܐܘ ܡܪܝ
ܡܢܐ ܐܡܪܬ ܀
ܐܝܬ ܗܘܐ
ܠܝ ܗܟܐ
ܒܪܢܫ ܦܫܠ
f. 25a ܕܟ̈ܘܦܝܢ :
ܘܦܠܛ ܠܟܢ
ܗܘܐ ܠܒܪ
ܠܐܟܫܢܐܝܢ ܀
ܘܝܗܒܐ
ܐܠܗܐ
ܠܘܒܕܘܝ
ܦܠܒܝܐ ܀ ܘܝܗܒ
ܠܗ ܒܘܬܪ
ܦܠܓ ܀ ܘܗܘ

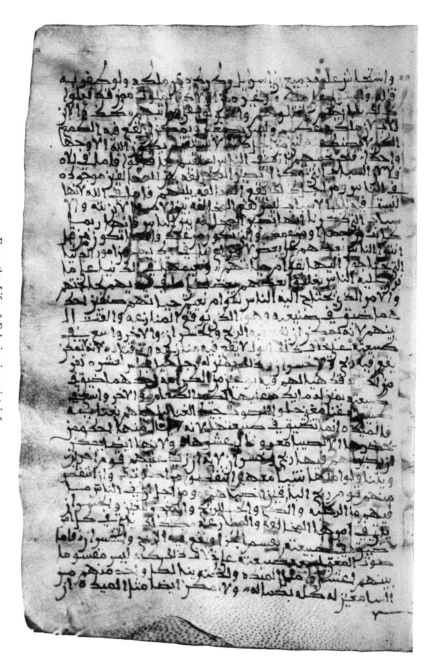

From the Life of Eulogios in script inf.
ff. 32b 25a in script sup.

f. 25a

الذي ظهر للناس من مريم [illegible]

[illegible] به وليس من ارض ومن اجل ذلك واله مثليه

وقد ضل الذي يسمون الجسد ولم يعقلوا بان كلمة الله [illegible]

المسيح في كل مكان لا يحوي عليه مكان وايضا فقد

وصفت الكتاب المسيح انه في كل مكان ولم يخلو منه مكان

ولا يحتوي عليه موضع قال النبي ان المسيح قال ان من يحبني و

حفظ هو كلمتي وان ابي يحبه ونحن ناتيه ونصنع عنده المسكن و

قال في موضع اخر انه الذي اجتمع اثنين او ثلثة على اسمي فانا

ثم بينهم الذي لا يدل ليس في المخلوق من يستطيع يكون في

كل مكان ولو كان المسيح ليس الا البشر الذي اخذ من مريم فقد

لم يوصف بذلك لان البشر محتوي وقد وصف الكتاب المسيح

هو ان وصف نفسه انه بين كل من يجتمع من اجل اسمه ومعروف ان

تجتمع من اجل اسمه في كل غداه وعشيه وساعات النهار و

الليل [illegible] في الحد [illegible] الناس في اقطار الارض

ولا يحدها وهو بينهم كما قال وايضا هو بين منعما

وصياما على ما قال وان بعد بعضهم عن بعض من حضر في الزمن طرفها

وابوه معه وسلكنهم فليس المسيح هذا الجسد الذي ظهر

فقط ولكنه ابن الله الباكر الذي هو مع ابيه في كل مكان

ولا يخلو منه مكان مثل ابيه ومن اجل ذلك فهو الله مثله

وقد ضل الذي يشكك من اجل انه اشتمل جسدا وقالته [illegible]

وسمى [illegible] الذي [illegible] للعباد الذي [illegible]

[illegible] يوحنا وايضا فقد وصف الكتاب

المسيح انه يعرف جميع سر [illegible] الانجيل ان المسيح حيث

كان في اورشليم في عيد الفصح [illegible] امنوا به لانهم

راوا العجائب التي كان يعمل ولم يكن يسوع [illegible] منهم ولا

يامنهم على نفسه لانه قد كان يعرف جميع الناس ولم يكن

يحتاج ان يشهد عنده على احد من الناس لانه قد كان يعلم

بان جميع الناس لكن لا يعلم جميع الناس من احد [illegible] مخلوق

ولو كان المسيح لم يكن الا هذا البشر المخلوق الذي [illegible]

من مريم فقد لم يوصف بذلك وقد وصف الكتاب المسيح

انه قد كان يعلم ذلك فالمسيح ليس هو هذا البشر الظاهر فقط

ولكنه [illegible] الذي يعرف جميع السر من

ابيه ومن اجل ذلك [illegible] فقد ضل من شك فيه ولا يعلم

الله اليه ولا [illegible] نفسه

f. 32a ܫܡܥ: ܘܠܐ
ܢܣܒ ܠܗ̇ܝ
ܐܢܐ: ܘܣܒܝܬ
ܠܗ: ܘܐܫܟܚܬ
ܚܕܐ ܣܒܐ
ܘܐܡܪܬ ܠܗ̇:
ܒܗܝܡܢ
ܐܝܟܢܐ ܗܘ
ܠܗ ܬܠܬܐ
ܒܦ̈ܬܓܡ
ܕܐܝܟܘܠ
ܐܢܐ ܒܟܡ:
f. 25b ܕܠܐ ܐܚܠܝܬ
ܡܟܪ̇ܝ ܟܠܗܘܢ:
ܘܐܡܪܬ ܠܗ
ܐܢܐ ܝܗܒܐ
ܠܟ: ܘܐܙܠܬ
ܘܐܝܬܝܬ
ܠܗ ܒܢܫܘܠ
ܘܠܒܫ
ܘܝܬܒܬ
ܠܗ̇ ܥܡܗ:

f. 32a ܘܫܪܝܐܬ
ܡܡܠܠܐ
ܠܗ ܡܠܝܢ
ܕܗܘܝܐ
ܘܐܡܪܐ ܠܗ
ܠܝܬ ܐܢܬ
ܡܕܡ ܕܦܠܠܐ
ܐܢܬ: ܘܠܐ
ܝܕܥ ܠܟ ܕܝ
ܕܬܝܬܐ
ܠܡܪܬܐ:
ܠܝܬ ܐܢܬ
f. 25b ܡܕܡ ܕܡܫܝܢܝܢܐ
ܒܟܐ ܫܪܝܟܘܬܐ:
ܘܡܠܝܢ
ܣܘܪ̈ܚܢܐ:
ܝܕܥ ܐܡܪܬ
ܠܗ: ܘܐܢܐ
ܐܡܪܬ
ܘܡܢܐ ܐܢܬܝ
ܫܐܡܐ
ܕܢܟܟܢ:

f. 11b ܐܘܠܘܓܝܘܣ܀
ܘܒܬܪ
ܙܒܢܝܢ
ܫܡܥܬ ܕܝܢ
ܒܘܫܢܐ، ܕܓܢܪ.
ܠܐܘܠܘܓܝܘܣ܀
ܘܐܦܩܗ
ܡܢ ܩܘܕܡ
ܚܝܠܘܗܝ
ܕܗܦܛܠܝܐ
ܘܒܪ ܐܘܢ
ܐܬܒܢܝܬ
f. 12a ܐܣܛܪܛܝܬ
ܘܝ ܠܗ
ܠܡܠܟܐ
ܘܠܒܘܫܐ
ܕܐܘܟܕܢܬ
ܠܢܦܫܗ܀
ܘܗܘܝ ܐܢܐ
ܗܘܝܬ ܬܡܢ
ܒܫܡܫܬܐ
ܡܫܡܫܬ

f. 11b ܘܫܡܥܬ
ܡܘܠܦܢ
ܕܦܢܝ
ܘܐܬܡܨܪܬ
ܠܗܘ ܓܝܠܝܐ
ܕܒܟܐ ܗܘܬ
ܠܐܘܠܘܓܝܘܣ
ܘܐܬܒܬ ܒܗ
ܗܘܝܬ ܐܢܐ
ܕܡܬܒܢܡ
ܒܒܢܝܢܬܐ
ܕܐܪܥܘܗܝ܀
f. 12a ܘܗܘܝܬ
ܡܚܬܪ
ܕܝ ܐܢܐ
ܐܘܠܘܓܝܘܣ
ܗܘܝ ܐܘܠ
ܫܢܝܬܝ
ܘܟܠܗ ܐܢܫܐ܀
ܒܪ ܕܝ
ܗܘܐ ܪܡܫܐ
ܘܫܡܫܬ

f. 11a ܘܒܛܠ ܗܘܐ
ܥܒܕܐ
ܛܒܐ ܕܗܘܐ
ܥܒܕ܀ ܘܢܦܩ
⌜ܐܠܦ⌝ ܘܦܪܫ
ܠܦܝܠܘܣܘܦܘܬܗ܀
ܗܘܐ ܕܝ
ܒܐܗܘ
ܡܪܘܣܐ
ܡܠܟܐ
ܘܣܦܝܢܘܗ
f. 12b ܡܠܝ܀ ⌜ܒ⌝ܪܗ
ܕܣܦܝܢܘܗ܀
ܘܦܪܒ
ܐܘܠܨܢܗ
⌜ܠ⌝ܡܠܟܐ
ܕܗܒ ܗܘ
ܘܠܟܠ
ܪ̈ܒܢܘܗܝ
ܕܡܠܟܐ
ܠܒܝܬ
ܕܐܬܥܒܕ

f. 11a ܐܦܪܥܘܗ
ܥܠ ܟܘܠ
ܐܦܪܥܢܐ܀
ܘܐܡ
ܐܘܣܝܐ
ܪܒܐ ܗܕܐ
ܕܡܬܦܪܢܐ
ܕܡܢܪܢܐ܀
ܒܕܡܐ
ܠܘܡܕܢ܀
ܘܗܘܐ
f. 12b ܡܢ ܒܬܪ
ܬܪ̈ܬܝܢ
ܫ̈ܢܝܢ ܣܡܝܬ
ܬܘܒܢ
ܒܝܠܡܗ
ܠܗܘ ܛܠܝܐ
ܒܡܫܝܬܐ
ܡܕܫܬܐ܀
ܘܐܡܪܝܬ
ܒܢܦܫܝ
ܐܪܐ ܗܝ ܗܘ

f. 24b ܠܒܢ̈ܝܬܗ ܗܘܝ
ܡܫܝܚܝܬܐ
ܕܠܗ ܀ ܘܗܘܐ
ܒܪ ܐܢܫ
ܒܦܓܪܐ:
ܘܫܡܥ ܗܘܝ
ܗܠܝܢ
ܕܒܠܘܬ ܀
ܘܐܫܬܡܥ
ܢܩܘܒ ܚܕ
ܕܟܘܪ ܀ ܘܬܘܩܦ
f. 23a ܐܢܫ ܘܐܫܬܡܥ
ܡܕܝܪܐ
ܡܠܟܐ ܕܗܒ ܀
ܘܒܟܡ ܬܡܗܘ ܀
ܘܐܡܪ ܗܘܢ
ܕܗܒܐ ܡܢ
ܕܒܢ̈ܝ
ܐܝܣܪܐܝܠ
ܗܘ ܀ ܡܠܟܐ
ܐܘܢ ܝܒܒܕ ܀
ܐܢ ܝܫܒ

f. 24b ܝܬܗ ܠܡܪ̈ܬܐ
ܫܡܥ ܗܘ
ܐܪܒܘܢܐ
ܘܢܣܒ ܠܗ ܀
ܘܐܢܐ ܐܘܦ
ܒܡܢܝܢܘܗ
ܪܒ ܐܢܐ
ܢܦܠ ܀ ܐܠܐ
ܢܣܒ ܝܬܗ
ܠܐܬܪ
ܚܘܪܢ ܗܢ
f. 23a ܕܠܝܬ ܐܢܫ
ܡܒܪ ܠܝ ܀
◯ܒܟܡ ܕܝ
ܐܒܪ ܒܟ̈ܠܝܡ
ܗܘܝܢ ܕܫܒܩܘܢ
ܒܬܒܝܡ ܀
ܘܒܠܠܝܐ
ܦܒܝ ܕܗܒܐ
ܘܐܝܒܠ ܝܬܗ
ܠܡܦܪܗ
ܕܢܗܪܐ ܀

Cf. *Z.D.M.G.* LVI. pp. 259, 260.

f. 24a ܡܢ ܩܕܡ ܐܘܪ̈ܕܐ܆
ܠܬܒܥܐ ܠܬܗ܀
ܒܪ̇ܢ ܕ̇ܝ
ܐܘܣܦ ܠܗ
ܒܪ̇ܒܐ܀
ܘܡܫܚܬ ܬܪ̈ܝܢ
ܡܫܝܚܘܢ
ܕܗܘܘ ܡܩ̈ܠܝܢ
ܒܒܘܒܗ
ܕܐܘܠܘܓܝܣ
ܒܘܬܪ ܦܓܪ܀
f. 23b ܘܒܟܠ ܡܟܐ
ܕܗܘܘ ܡܩ̈ܠܝܢ
ܗܘܐ ܡܡܒܠ
ܒܒܘܒܗ܀
ܘܐܬܒܪܬ
ܘܫܒܚܬ ܠܬܗ
ܠܐܠܗܐ܀
ܪ̇ܚ ܡܠܘܢ
ܐܘܠܘܓܝܣ
ܕܝ ܢܦܫ

f. 24a ܡܐܟ ܡܢ
ܫܒܝܗ܀
ܘܫܕ̇ܪ ܠܘܬܝ
ܗܘ ܓܠܠܐ
ܚܕ ܡܢ ܗܠܝܢ
ܕܡܐܡܢܝܢ
ܘܡܕܡܘܢ܆
ܘܐܡܠ ܠܬܝ
ܠܓܒܗ ܘܐܡܪ̇
ܠܝ܀ ܐܬ ܗܘ
ܕܒܪ̇ܒܬ
f. 23b ܒܐܘܠܘܓܝܣ܀
ܘܒܬ̈ܘ ܒܒܠ
ܗܠܝܢ ܕܡܐܡܢܝܢ
ܘܐܡܪ̇ܘ ܐܝܢ
ܡܪ̇ܢ܀ ܘܬܘܒܢ
ܐܡܪ̇
ܐܡܘ̈ܪܘ ܠܗ
ܕܒܪ̇ܒܬܟ
ܬܬܒܥܐ܀
ܘܐܡܪ̇ܬ
ܐܝܢ ܡܪ̇ܝ܆

This is the leaf published by Schulthess, *Z.D.M.G.* LVI. p. 258.

f. 68b ܠܗ ܗܘܝܢ
ܕܡܣܟܢ ܐܘܦ
ܠܣܘ̈ܥܪܢ ܀
ܘܐܡܪ ܠܗ
ܠܟ ܐܝܬ ܗܘ ܀
ܘܐܡܪܬ
ܠܗ ܐܢܐ
ܒܟܐ ܡܢܝܢ
ܡܪܝ ܗܒ ܠܗ
ܗܘܝܢ ܕܒܘܠ
ܒܢ̈ܝܫܐ
f. 69a ܢܫ̈ܒܘܩ
ܠܒܢܝܢ
ܘܢܫܐ
ܠܒܪܘܠܗ ܀
ܘܐܡܪ ܠܗ
ܐܢܐ ܐܡܪܬ
ܠܝ ܕܠܒ ܐܝܬ
ܗܘ ܀ ܐ ܕ
ܒܟܐ ܐܝܬ
ܕܠܝܬ ܠܗ
ܚܘܒ ܠܗ

f. 68 b ܒܢܦܫܗ ܕܗܘ
ܡܫܬܘܕܐ
ܒܡ̈ܣܟܢܐ
ܦܓ̈ܝܢܐ ܀
ܘܐܢܐ ܝܗܒ
ܠܗ ܀ ܟܡ
ܐܡܪܬ ܠܗ :
ܗܢ ܒܢ
ܐܚ̈ܐ، ܒܟܝ
ܢܦܫܗ ܀
ܘܝܗܒܬ
f. 69a ܗܘܝܢ ܕܐܡܪ
ܦܐ̈ܡܝܢ
ܒܡܪܬܝ
ܡܝܐܡܬܐ
ܡܕܝܢܬܐ ܀
ܘܗܘܐ ܚܕ
ܦܠܓܐ ܗܘܐ
ܝܗܒ ܟܠ
ܒܝܦܐ
ܡܕܝܢܬܐ ܀
ܘܐܘܠܘܓܝܣ

f. 68a ܐܟܣܢܝܘܬܟ :
ܐܢܐ ܕܝ
ܟܕ ܐܬܝܬ
ܠܥܠܝܬܝ
ܘܙܒܢܬ
ܕܒܝܪܗ
ܕܓܒܪܐ
ܡܢܐܬܪܐ :
ܓܐܡܪܬ
ܬܪ̈ܬܝܢ
ܙܘܙ̈ܝܢ :
f. 69b ܘܐܫܬܟܚܬ
ܠܐܠܗܐ
ܗܘܝܬ ܕܡܠܠ
ܠܗ ܒܪܒܬܐ :
ܕܗܒܬ ܠܗ ܚܝܐ
ܠܐܢ̈ܫܐ
ܗܘܝܬ ܕܫܒܩ :
ܘܟܕ ܓܐܡܪܬ
ܕܝ ܬܠܬ
ܙܘܙ̈ܝܢ
ܗܘܝܬ ܪܒܢܐ

f. 68a ܗܘܝܬ ܡܚܝܬ
ܡܥܘܬܪ ܥܪ
ܡܢ ܡܘܟܐ :
ܘܫܒܩܬ
ܐܢܐ ܐܢܫ
ܕܐܬܐ ܠܘܬܝ
ܒܐܘܟܣܢܝܐ
ܡܢܐܘܪܚܐ
ܘܐܡܪ ܠܝ
ܡܢܐ ܠܟ ܕܢܝܚܐܝܬ :
ܘܐܡܪܬ
f. 69b ܡܪܝ ܡܠܟܐ
ܡܗܝܡܢܬ
ܠܡܫܝܚܐ
ܕܠܐ ܡܟܐܠ
ܠܝܫ ܟܕ
ܡܟܐ ܕܡܫܬܘܒ
ܡܢܝ ܠܓܠܠ
ܐܘܠܓܝܣ
ܡܦܠܓܐ
ܕܒܩ̈ܝܐ :
ܕܗܒܬ ܠܝ ܡܬܠ

f. 80 b ⌜ܗܘ ܡܬܡܪ⌝ ܀
ܘܐܘ⌜ܡܢ⌝ܘܬܗ
ܦܠܚ ܒܝܘܡ ܀
ܘܗܘ ܥܡܠ
ܒܟܘܠ ܝܘܡ
ܒܚܕ ܩܝܛ
ܘܣܬܘ ܥܕ
ܡܐ ܠܪܡܫܐ
ܕܠܐ ܛܥܡ
ܟܠܘܡ ܀
ܘܒܪܡܫܐ
f. 75 a ܗܘ ܐܬܐ
ܠܩܪܝܬܐ
ܘܟܘܠ ܐܟܣܢܝ
ܕܗܘ ܡܫܟܚ
ܗܘ ܢܣܒ ܠܗ
ܠܒܝܬܗ
ܘܡܫܡܫ ܠܗܘܢ ܀
ܘܡܟܐ ܕܝ
ܕܡܫܬܪ̈ܝܢ
ܗܘ ܡܗܒ
ܠܟܠ̈ܒܐ ܥܕ

f. 80 b ܗܟܐ ܠܢܘܡܕܢ
ܘܐܝܬ ܗܘ
ܢܘܡܕܢ ܒܪ
ܗܟܐ ܘܒܣܪܝܡ
ܥܒܝܡ ܀ ܘܗܘܐ
ܥܡܠ ܒܟܘܠ
ܝܘܡ ܒܚܕ
ܩܝܛ ܀ ܥܕ
ܕܝ ܗܘܝܬ
ܛܠܐ ܡܘܕܡ
ܐܪ̈ܒܥܝܢ ܫܢ̈ܝܢ ܀
f. 75 a ܫܠܡܝܬ
ܕܝܘܡ ܒܥܒܕܬܐ
ܕܐܢ̈ܕܐܝ
ܒܩܪܝܬܐ
ܗܕܐ ܕܗܘ̈ܠܝܢ
ܒܗ̇ ܀ ܘܒܪܡܫܐ
ܐܬܐ ܘܕܒܪ
ܠܗ̇ ܘܠܐܟܣ̈ܢܝܐ
ܕܗܘܘ ܒܡܫܐ
ܗܘܝܢ ܦܘܢܕܩܝܬܐ
ܕܠܗ ܘܐܢܫ

f. 80a ܕܝܒܬܘܫ
ܘܐܙܠ ܠܗ
ܘܪܗܛ ܐܘܣܝܡ
ܘܝܕ ܠܬܗ
ܘܫܪܝ܆ ܡܒܥܐܡ
ܠܗ ܘܐܡܪ܀
ܚܝ ܗܘ
ܐܠܗܐ
ܕܠܝܬ ܐܢܐ
ܥܒܕ ܠܬܟ
ܒܪ ܟܐ
ܕܬܬܟܐܢܘܪ
f. 75b ܠܐ ܦܢ ܗܘ
ܗܘ ܫܒܥܐ܀
ܠܐ ܓܪ ܗܘܐ
ܐܢܫ ܡܕܠ
ܕܣܒܥܐ
ܠܣܒܥܐ ܡܬܝܪܦ܀
ܕܗܘܐ ܡܣܟܢ
ܠܗ ܣܓܝ܀
ܘܟܕ ܐܡܪ
ܠܗ܆ ܒܒܝ ܠܐ

f. 80a ⌜ܕ⌝ܐܒܘ⌜ܠܬܐ⌝
⌜ܘܒܬܪܟܢ⌝ ܐܢܐ
ܐܡܪ ܠܟ܀
ܘܟܢ ܕܐܟܠ
ܫܒܥܐ ܐܡܪ
ܠܐܢܫ܆ ܠܐ
ܬܗܘܐ ܘܒܥܐ
ܡܕܠ ܠܒܕܠ
ܓܪ ܕܗܘܝ ܐܬ
ܢܣܒ ܒܟܣܐ ܠܐ
ܐܡܪܬ ܠܟ
ܒܪ ܗܘܦܟܝܢ
f. 75b ܡܬܦܪܢܝܢ
ܒܡܪܬܐ܆
ܘܠܐ ܓܠܝܬ
ܠܟ܆ ܐܘܦ ܐܬ
ܠܐ ܬܬܬܢܐ
ܠܐܢܫ ܟܐ
ܕܐܢܐ ܐܡܪ
ܠܟ܆ ܘܐܡܪ ܠܗ
ܗܪ ܫܒܥܐ
ܐܘܠܓܢܐ

f. 2b ܠܐܣܘܢ ܟܠ ܦܠܓ
ܡܢܐܬܪ̈ܬܐ
ܕܡܕܢ̈ܚܐ
ܣܓܝ܆ ܘܠܐ
ܓܒܐ ܣܒܐ
ܕܓܠܝܼܐ ܠܗ
ܠܐܣܘܢ ܡܢ ܦܠܓ
ܘܗ̇ܘ ܣܒܐ܆
ܘܒܡ ܐܬܒܢܝܐܘ
ܐܣܘܢ ܘܠܐ
ܡܠܠ ܥܡ ܣܒܐ.
ܒܪ ܡܢܐ ܕܐܬܐ
f. 7a ܠܐܣܩܝܛܝܣ܆
ܒܪ ܕܝ ܐܬܐ
ܐܣܘܢ ܠܘܬܗ܆
ܠܐ ܐܘܟܠ
ܠܣܒܐ
ܕܢܐܟܘܠ ܗܘܢ
ܣܝܒܘܬܐ
ܕܠܗ
ܕܟܝܢ ܟܣܦܝ
ܥܒ̈ܕܝܢ ܗܘܐ

f. 2b ܣܒܐ ܐܟܠ
ܟܘܠ ܝܘܡܐ
ܫܢ̈ܘܗܝ܆
ܒܪ ܕܝ ܗܘܐ
ܪܡܫܐ: ܐܬܐ
ܣܒܐ ܠܘܬ
ܐܣܘܢ ܘܐܡܪ.
ܠܣܒܐ ܒܪܝ
ܒܪܝ ܥܡܘܬ
ܐܟܘܬܟ ܕܢܦܩܘܬ
ܡܢ ܟܦܢܐ܆
ܘܐܡܪ: ܠܝܬ
f. 7a ܠܐ ܐܒ: ܐܠܘ
ܟܢ ܗܘܐ ܠܝ
ܐܒ ܐܝܬ
ܗܘܐ ܪܚܡ
ܠܒܪܗ܆
ܘܣܒܐ ܐܡܪ
ܠܗ: ܐܝܟܢ
ܗܘܝ ܒܫܠܡ܆
ܘܓܪ ܣܒܐ
ܬܪܒܐ

f. 2a ܘܠܐ ܗܘܐ
ܥܒܕ ܠܟܦܘܪܐ
ܟܠܗܘܢ: ܘܕܒܪ
ܠܥܡܐ
ܟܠܫܘܕܘܝ
ܘܬܒܥ ܠܗܘܢ
ܡܥܠܠܝܢ
ܦܠܚܘܢ
ܒܡ ܦܠܚ
ܠܡܫܬܗ̇
ܕܢܥܒܐ:
f. 7b ܒܕܡ̈ܟܝܢ ܗܟܢ
ܒܕܡܐ ܠܟܦܘܪܐ:
ܘܒܟܦܘܪܐ
ܕܝ ܥܠܬܗ
ܦܠܚܘܢ
ܠܦܠܚ: ܘܐܪ̈ܬܐ
ܒܐܘܪܚܐ:
[1]ܘܡܢ ܕ⌜ܐ⌝ܪ̈ܬܝܢ[1]
ܒܐܘܪܚܐ:
ܒܒܪ ܐܣܘܢ
ܡܬܦܘܫܐ

f. 2a ܠܐܒܘܗ ܕܠܗܘܢ
ܘܐܡܪ: ܒܒܪ
ܚܒܐ ܐܒܐ
ܘܐܡܘܪ
ܠܝ ܡ̇ܢ ܗܘ
ܗ̇ܘ ܫܒܐ:
ܘܡܢ ܗ̣ܘ
ܐܬ ܡܒܪ ܠܗ:
ܘܠܐ ܝܕܥܐ
ܫܒܐ ܕܢܡܘܪ
ܠܗ: ܬܘܒܢ
f. 7b ܐܣܘܢ ܒܒܪ
ܡܬܦܘܫܐ
ܡܫܒܫ ܠܗ
ܘܐܡܪ: ܫܟܪ
ܦܬܚ ܟܠ ܐܬ
ܠܝ ܐܒܐ:
ܘܟܠ ܦܬܚ ܗܕܐ
ܠܝܬ ܐܬ
ܟܠܐ ܠܝ ܐܒܐ:
ܗܘܐ ܟܪ
ܐܡ̇ܪ ܠܗ

1–1 Cod. ܘܡܢ ܟܐܪ̈ܬܝܢ

f. 67a ܘܟܒܪܐ ܘܫܠܡ
ܠܬܠܡܝܕܗ
ܘܐܡܪ ܠܗܘܢ ܀
ܐܢ ܐܢܬ
ܐܬܘܢ ܫܐܠ̈ܝܢ
ܡܪܐ ܐ̈ܬܘ
ܥܡܝ ܠܒܝܬܝ ܀
ܘܗܘܐ ܕܝ
ܠܚܡ ܐܘܦ
ܦܫܛܐ ܕܗܘܐ
ܒܗ ܒܘܝܢܐ ܀
ܘܗܘܐ ܣܓܝ
f. 70b ܒܗ ܒܫܘܒܚܐ
ܕܡܪܬܐ
ܘܟܠܐ ܐܟܣܢܝܢ ܀
ܘܐܡܪ ܠܣܒܐ
ܘܠܬܠܡܝܕܗ
ܘܟܘܠ ܐܟܣܢܝܢ
ܕܐܬܝܢ
ܘܐܡܪ
ܝܬܗܘܢ
ܠܒܝܬܗ

f. 67a ܘܐܫܝܓ
ܪ̈ܓܠܝܗܘܢ
ܕܐܚ̈ܝܐ
ܘܕܣܒܐ ܀
ܠܐ ܕܝ ܗܘܐ
ܠܗ ܐܝܟ
ܒܒܝܬܗ
ܐܘܦ ܠܐ
ܒܐܬܪ ܣܘܪ̈ܢ
ܐܠܐ ܐܠܗܐ
ܒܠܚܘܕ ܀
ܘܐܫܝܓ
f. 70b ܦܬܘܪܐ
ܘܩܕܡܝܗܘܢ ܀
ܘܒܪ ܩܨ̈ܒܐ
ܢܩܒ ܩܝ̈ܬܐ
ܘܝܗܒ
ܝܬܗܘܢ
ܠܚܠ̈ܫܝܐ
ܕܩܪܬܐ ܀
ܗܟܕܝܢ ܥܠ
ܗܘܐ ܥܒܕ ܀

f. 67 b ܗܦܟܐ ܡܢܟ
ܒܪܘܚܐ
ܕܐܬܐ
ܐܘܠܘܓܝܣ
ܡܢ ܐܣܩܝܛܝܐ
ܠܐܬܪܘܬܗ
ܘܡܫܝܚܬܐ ܀
ܘܠܒܝܠ ܒܢ̈ܝ
ܗܘܐ ܗܦܟܐ
ܡܬܚܙܐ ܠܗ ܀
ܗܘ ܐܚܘܢ
ܕܝ ܠܐ
f. 70 a ܗܘܐ ܕܝܢ
ܗܟܐ ܗܝ
ܡܫܡܫܬܐ ܀
ܘܒܬܪ
ܬܡܢܝܢ
ܬܡܢ ܒܕܡܐ
ܠܫܡܥܐ
ܕܠܐ ܐܬ̈ܠܘ
ܘܠܐ ܐܝܬ̈ܘ
ܘܒܪܝ ܐܚܘܢ

f. 67 b ܢܚܬ ܚܕ
ܗܦܟܐ ܘܐܬܟܪܝ ܀
ܐܘ ܕܒܒܪܗ
ܐܬ ܕܟܪ ܢ
ܠܒܪܝܠܝܢ ܗܘܐ
ܠܗ ܕܡܫܘܬܐ ܀
ܘܡܟܐ ܕܗܘܘ
ܡܟܠܠܝܢ ܀
ܐܬܐ ܚܕ
ܗܟ ܒܪ
ܠܟ ܐܪܝܢ
ܒܫܘܡܬܗ
f. 70 a ܘܟܠ ܫ̈ܒܘ
ܘܪܝܫܗ ܫܘܪ
ܘܓܒܝܢ ܡܢ
ܫܒܘܬܗ
ܘܟܕ ܕܝ
ܫܡܥܐ ܠܐܟܐ
ܕܫܐܝܠ
ܪܗܛ ܘܓܦ *
ܗܘ ܘܒܪܝ
ܟܒܪܘ ܠܗ

f. 34b ܒܐܠܗܐ
ܘܢܫܬܡ
ܠܣܘܪܐ ؛
ܘܟܕ ܡܟܠܗ
ܠܫܒܐ ܦܘܪܐ :
ܐܦܝܣ
ܫܒܐ ܠܗܠܝܢ
ܕܒܐܠܗܐ ؛
ܠܒܒܠ
ܕܐܡܪ ܗܒܐ
ܦܝܠܘܣ
ܐܝܬ ܠܝ
f. 39a ܕܢܝܟܬܪ
ܘܟܕܒܢ : ܘܦܪ̈ܘ
ܬܟܡ ؛ ܘܦܪܝ
ܬܠܟܢܕܗ
ܟܢܝܢ ܘܐܡܪ ؛
ܟܕ ܡܒܐ
ܠܐܡܬܝ
ܐܝܢ ܣܟܠܝܢ
ܢܐ̈ܪܠ[1] ܠܝ
ܠܐܣܝܣܬܝܣ ؛

f. 34b ܘܦܒܐ
ܐܡܪ ܠܐ.
ܐܠܐ ܗܒܐ
ܢܒܬܪ ܝܘܡܢ̈ ؛
ܘܝܬܒܘ ܠܗܘܢ
ܒܡܨܥܬܗ ܕܝ
ܕܦܘܪܬܐ ܗܝܟ
ܦܢ[ܝ]ܬܐ
ܕܐ[ܟ̈]ܦܢܝ ؛
○ܐܡ[ܪ] ܐܝܣܘܡ
ܠܫܒܐ : ܐܪܐ
ܙܐܦܪ ܗܘ
f. 39a ܠܐܠܗܐ
ܕܐܝܢ ܝܬܟ̈ܒܝܢ
ܗܝܟ ܙܟ̈ܘܠܝܢ ؛
ܢܐ̈ܪܠ[1] ܠܝ ܕܝ
ܠܟܪܦܝܢ ؛
○ܐܡܪ ܫܒܐ
ܠܐ ܐܠܐ
ܗܒܐ ܐܝܢ
ܝܬܒܝܢ ؛
ܗܘܐ ܠܝ

[1] Cod. ܢܐ̈ܪܠܘܢ *bis*

ܕܐܠܗܐ f. 34a
ܦܪܝܫܬ
ܬܗܘܘܢ
ܠܟܐܢܬ
ܠܬܫܒܘܚܬܗܘܢ
ܕܗܘ̈ܕܝܐ
ܘܟܪ̈ܣܛܝܢܐ :
ܕܐܬܠ ܠܝ
ܡܪܝ ܝܫܘܥ
ܫܘܠܡ ܟܬܒ
ܒܫܠܡܘܢ
ܒܡܠܟܘܬܗ
ܐܡܝܢ : f. 39b
< < < < < < <

ܥܠ ܚܝܘܗ ܕܐܟܣܢܝܐ
ܘܟܪ̈ܣܛܝܢܐ ܕܐܬܩ̈ܛܠܘ
ܟܠܦܪ ܚܝܠܐ ܘܟܪܝܬܘ
ܚܝܘܗܝ ܕܦܠܘܣܘ
ܘܗܘ ܕܐܠܟܣܢܕܪܝܐ :
ܕܟܪܘܙܘܢ ܕܝ
ܕܗܠܝܢ ܟܪ̈ܣܛܝܢܐ

ܡܬܠܒܒ ܒܪܘܡܒܪ f. 34a
ܫ̈ܝܢܐ ܕܪ̈ܘܡܝܢ
ܒܡ̈ܪܝܢ ܘܬܘܡܝܢܐ
ܕܡܪܐ ܒܝܠܬ̈ܗܘܢ
ܬܫܪܝܢ ܒܠܝܢ ܘܒܠ
ܒܘܠܗ ܒܠܝܢܐ ܐܡܝܢ :
< < < < < < < < <

ܒܝܘܡ ܕܐܘܠܘܦܣ
ܡܕܝܢܬܐ ܕܗܘܬ
ܡܠܟ ܒܬܘܟܢ :
ܐܚܪܢ ܐܒܐ f. 39b
ܕܝܢܐܠ
ܘܚܢܢܐ
ܕܐܣܘܡܬܗܘܢ :
ܕܐܠܝܬ
ܕܝܢ
ܠܬܠܡܐܝܗ
ܚܕ ܡܢ ܗܘ
ܬܠܡܝܕܐܝ
ܘܡܬܠܝܢ

f. 61b ܘܗܘܬ ܩܪܐ
ܒܩܘܠ ܪܒܐ
ܒܐܘܣܛܘܢܣܛܠܐ
ܕܣܛܪܛܝܘܛܐ
ܡܙܝܢ̈ܘܗܝ
ܕܡܫܝܚܐ :
ܘܡܬܒܣܡ
ܒܟܪܘܙܐ
ܕܐܬܠܠܦܘܬܗܘܢ :
ܘܒܩܘܠ ܒܪ
ܗܘܬ
ܡܫܒܚ
f. 60a ܠܐܠܗܐ
ܐܒܐ ܕܠܒܢܝܗ
ܒܟܠܐ :
ܗܘ ܕܠܗ
ܬܫܒܘܚܬܐ
ܠܥܠܡ ܥܠܡܝܢ
ܐܡܝܢ : :
ܫܠܡ ܕܝ
ܐܫܒܚܬ ܐܢܐ
ܘܫܢܝܢܘ

f. 61b ܒܪ̈ܚܡܘܗܝ
ܕܡܪܢ ܝܫܘܥ
ܡܫܝܚܐ
ܠܗ ܫܢܝܢܝ
ܦܐܪܘܗ ܥܠ
ܠܗ ܢܘܦܪ :
ܒܬܪ̈ܥܝܢ
ܒܠܫܢܐ
ܡܨܪ̈ܝܐ :
ܘܐܢܐ ܕܝ
ܒܫܘܕܗ
ܕܡܫܝܚܐ
f. 60a ܦܫܪܝܬ
ܬܗܘܢ
ܠܠܫܢܐ
ܝܘܢܝܐ :
ܕܗܘܬ
ܡܢ ܬܪܝܢ
ܠܫܢܝܐ
ܡܨܪ̈ܝܐ
ܘܝܘܢܝܐ
ܘܒܫܘܕܗ

f. 61 a ܘܥܘܒܕܝܢ
ܒܥܘܒܕܝܗܘܢ
ܐܡܝܢ ܀
ܘܢܫܒܚ
ܠܐܠܗܐ
ܘܢܘܕܐ ܠܗ
ܡܢ ܟܘܠܗ
ܢܦܫܢ ܗܕܢ
ܕܗܘܝ
ܪ̈ܚܡܘܝ
ܦܪܩ ܝܬܢ
f. 60 b ܡܢ ܒܝܢ
ܐܝܕܝܗܘܢ
ܕܒܥܠܕܒܒܝܢ
* * * *
* * * *
* * * *
* * * *
ܡܐܝܢ
* * * *
* * * *
* * * *

f. 61 a ܕܡܚܠܠ ܀
ܐܢܐ ܕܝ
ܐܡܘܢܝܣ
ܬܒܬ ܠܝ
ܠܡܣܪܝܢ
ܘܡܥܒܕ ܟܘܠ
ܗܠܝܢ ܕܬܒܥܐ
ܡܢ ܡܘܫܦ
ܒܪܢܫܐ
ܘܐܬܠܝܬ ܠܝ
ܠܡܣܪܝܢ
f. 60 b ܠܐ ܕܝ
ܠܐܬܪܝ
ܡܚܝܐ ܕ
ܕܫܝܡܘܗ
ܡܠܦܘܗ
ܐܠܐ ܦܪܝܢ
ܠܡܥܒܕܗ
* * * *
* * * *
* * * *
* * * *

f. 35b ܘܡܢ ܒܬܪ
ܒܗ̇ ܗܘ
ܡܫܒܪܢܗ
ܕܐܬܪܐ
ܐܟܢܐ ܕܗܠܝܢ
ܘܐܡܪ ܐܘ
ܚܒܝܒܝ
ܗܠܝܢ ܐܘܦ
ܡܢ̈ܒܝܐ
ܗܢܝܢ ܥܡܝܢ
ܕܡܫܝܚܐ
ܘܒܚܝ̈ܝܢ
f. 38a ܠܗ : ܒܟܪ̈ܘܗܝ
ܕܐܠܗܐ
ܐܬܒܟ̈ܪܘ :
ܘܫܐ̈ܘܝܢ
ܒܡܠܟܘܬܐ
ܕܫܡܝܐ :
ܘܡܢ ܒܬܪ
ܐܠܨܘܗܝ :
ܘܬܟܬܫܘܗܝ
ܘܫܢܩܘܗܝ

f. 35b ܠܘܬ ܡܪܢ
ܘܒܥܘܢ
ܟܠܝܠܐ
ܕܣܗܕܘܬܗܘܢ :
ܘܗܘܐ ܟܪ
ܗܢܘܢ ܡܬܒܢܝܢ
ܒܬܫܒܘܚܐ ܕܠܐ
ܡܬܡܠܠܐ :
ܐܝܢ ܕܝ
ܢܗܘܘܢ
ܘܢܚܘܦ
ܠܢܦܫܢ :
f. 38a ܘܠܗܘܢ
ܕܢܦܫܗ
ܕܡܒܘܒܘܢ
ܡܢ ܡܪܢ
ܫܘܫܘܗ
ܟܠ ܕܠܥܠܡ
ܕܡܒܒܕ ܠܬܢ
ܫܐܘܢ
ܐܘܦ ܐܢܢ
ܒܡܠܟܘܬܐ

f. 35a ܩܪܘܗ ܀
ܘܠܐ ܕܝ
ܒܬܪܝܬ
ܠܒܕܠ
ܚܪܒܗ
ܕܐܬܪܐ ܀
ܐܠܐ ܐܢܐ
ܡܢ ܩܘܫܬ
ܐܡܪܝܬ
ܠܟܘܢ ܡܢܐ
ܕܐܬܒܥܕ
ܬܡܢ ܀ ܐܘܦ
f. 38b ܐܬܘܢ ܕܝ
ܐܡܪܘ ܠܝ
ܡܢܐ ܐܬܒܥܕ
ܠܟܘܢ
ܡܢ ܩܘܫܬ
ܒܗܠܝܢ
ܕܐܬܛܠܠܘ
ܒܢܐ ܀ ܘܐܡܪܝܢ
ܠܗ ܒܘܠܐ
ܡܢ ܩܘܫܬ

f. 35a ܗܝܟ ܡܢܐ
ܕܐܬܒܥܕ
ܠܘܬܢ
ܘܦܐܪܘܒܢܐ ܀
○ܬܡܗܘܢ
ܕܝ ܥܠ
ܬܡܗܘܝ
ܕܐܠܗܐ ܀
ܕܗܒܕܢ ܒܗ
ܒܝܘܡܐ
ܒܘܠܗܘܢ
ܡܕܪܫܝܐ
f. 38b ܕܒܢܐ ܘܕܒܢܐ
ܐܬܒܠܠܘ
ܫܘܝܐܝܬ ܀
ܘܬܘܒ
ܕܒܡܢܝܢ
ܕܝ ܗܘܘ
ܘܪܬܚܝܢ
ܒܒܘܒܢܐ
ܥܠ ܗܠܝܢ
ܕܐܬܡܠܠܝܢ ܀

f. 48b ܠܡܪܢܐ
ܝܫܘܥ
ܡܫܝܚܐ ܀
ܗܘ ܕܠܗ
ܬܫܒܘܚܬܐ
ܠܥܠܡ ܥܠܡܝܢ
ܐܡܝܢ ܀ ܀
ܐܒܐ ܕܝ
ܐܚܪܢܐ
ܘܐܒܐ
ܐܘܪܝܢ
ܒܬܪ̈ܘ ܬܡܢ
f. 41a ܒܐܬܪܐ ܀
ܦܠܝܚܝܢ ܕܝ
ܒܫܒܬܗܘܢ
ܕܐܪ̈ܠܘܢ ܐܦ
ܕܒܬܪ̈ܘܢ ܀
ܐܢܐ ܕܝ ܕܠܐ
ܗܘܝܬ ܥܠ
ܡܫܘܒܪ
ܠܫܘܢܐ
ܕܝܪ̈ܒܢܗ

f. 48b ܕܐܬܪܐ
ܗܘ̇ ܀ ܘܠܐ
ܕܢܫܒܘܩ
ܡܢ ܝܩܘܬܐ
ܕܐܒܗ̈ܬܐ
ܕܐܬܩ̈ܘܦܠܘ ܬܡܢ ܀
ܐܬܡܫܒܚܬ
ܕܐܢܬܐ̇
ܠܝ ܠܘܬ
ܡܕܝܢܬܗܘܢ ܀
ܘܫܦܝܪ ܗܘܐ
ܪܚܡܗ
f. 41a ܕܡܫܝܚܐ
ܒܡܕܝܢܬܗ
ܡܫܡܫ
ܠܝ ܕܡܒܬܪ
ܒܐܬܪܐ ܀
ܘܐܡܪ ܠܝ
ܐܢܐ ܢܩܦ
ܠܟ ܀ ܘܡܫܠܡܐ
ܐܢܐ ܢܦܪܩܟ
ܒܟܘܠ

f. 48a ܡܪ̈ܥܝܬܐ
ܬܠ̈ܬܝܢ
ܘܬܫ̈ܥܐ ܀
*ܕܡܫܢܘܢܘܗ
ܕܝ ܕܗܘܐ
ܡܢ ܪܘܡܐ ܀
ܗܘܬ ܢܦܫܗ
ܒܗ ܒܗܘ
ܒܠܒܘܗ ܀
ܘܒܟܠ ܗܠܝܢ
ܕܐܬ̈ܬܚܣܘ
ܬܡܢ: ܢܦ̈ܫܗܘ
f. 41b ܫܒ̈ܩܝܢ
ܕܕܩ̈ܠܝܢ
ܘܐܬ̈ܐܘ
*ܠܐܪܘܣܘܬܘܢ
ܕܡܪ̈ܥܝܬܐ ܀
ܘܒܬܫܒܝܚܐ
ܘܒܐܝܩܪ
ܡܒܪ̈ܟܝܢ
ܠܗܘܢ ܀
ܠܒܥܠܗܘܢ

f. 48a ܒܐܬܪ ܚܕ
ܡܪܝܒ
ܠܡܣܟܪܘܢ ܀
ܕܘܡܫܟܘܗ
ܕܝ ܒܪܡܫܐ
ܡܫܬ ܀
ܘܡܒܪ̈ܟܝܢ
ܫܬܗ ܠܐ ܕܝ
ܒܡ ܡܪ̈ܥܝܬܐ ܀
ܐܠܐ ܡܪܝܒ
ܠܗܘܢ ܀
ܟܠܬܐ ܕܝ:
f. 41b ܕܠܐ ܢܦܬܘܚ
ܡܒܪܐ
ܘܢܚܒܒ
ܒܘܟ̈ܝܗܘܢ
ܕܡܪ̈ܥܝܬܐ ܀
ܒܡܫܗܘܢ
ܕܝ ܗܘ
ܡܬܟܢܫܐ ܀
ܐܪ̈ܒܥܝܢ
ܡܣܪ̈ܩܝܢ

* sic in Cod.

f. 66b ܕܝܢ ܘܫܠܝܘܢ
ܒܡܟܪܝܢܘܬܗ
ܕܝ ܪܓܫܗ
ܕܦܪܢ ܒܗܡ
ܕܒܪ̈ܒܢܝܐ
ܪܦܪܢ ܃ ܐܬ̈ܠܘ
ܡܐܢ̈ܝܢ
ܡܢܐܗ̈ܪܝܢ
ܕܪ̈ܚܡܝܢ ܃ ܘܡܦܩܘ
ܦܘܠܚ̈ܢܗܘܢ
ܕܡܕܒ̈ܪܢܐ ܃
f. 71a ܕܐܘܦ ܗܘܢ
ܢܨ̈ܚܢܗܘܢ
Matt. 25.36 ܡܠܟܐ: ܕܥܪܛܠܝ
ܗܘܝܬ
ܘܐܠܒܫܬܘܢ
ܠܝ ܃
ܕܘܡܫܘܗ
ܕܝ ܗܘܐ
ܗܡ ܪܘܡܐ ܃
ܘܗܘܘ ܕܝ

f. 66b ܥܠ ܐܪܒܥܐ ܃
ܐܝܟ ܕܝ
ܗܘܝܢ ܒܕܚܠܐ
ܪܒܐ ܃ ܢܨ̈ܚܝܢ
ܡܢܨܚܬܐ
ܕܠ̈ܦܘ
ܦܘܠܚ̈ܢܗܘܢ
ܕܡܕܒ̈ܪܢܐ
ܒܒ̈ܪܘܝ
ܕܡܫܝܚܐ ܃
ܗܠܝܢ ܐܘܢ
ܕܚܝ̈ܠܗܘܢ
f. 71a ܥܒܪܘ
ܠܡܫܝܚܐ:
ܘܒܫܘܠܡܗܘܢ
ܢܨܚܘ
ܐܪܒܥܐ
ܕܟܘܪ̈ܗܘܢ ܃
ܕܒܥ
ܡܬ̈ܦܪܢܝܐ
ܩܕ̈ܝܫܐ
ܫܬܠܡܘܢ

f. 66a ܒܬܪ ܕܐܬ̈ܠܗ
ܠܥܠܡܝܢ܆
ܘܫܒܩܘ
ܦܓܪ̈ܝܗܘܢ
ܥܠ ܩܒܪܗ
ܕܡܝܬܐ
ܠܫܘܬܐ
ܕܐܪܥܐ
ܘܠܚ̈ܝܘܬܐ
ܕܫܘܡܠܝܐ܆
ܗܠܝܢ ܕܝ
ܕܐܬܩ̈ܛܠܘ
f. 71b ܡܢܗܘܢ
ܒܢܫܘ ܕܝ
ܡܬܗܘܢ
ܘܒܢܒܘ
ܟܠܗܘܢ
ܐܒܠ ܪܒ܆
ܘܡܒܪ̈ܘ
ܡܬܗܘܢ
ܬܘܣܬ
ܛܘܪܐ ܠܟܠ

f. 66a ܡܢ ܡܕܒܪ̈ܝܐ
ܕܡܠ̈ܟܐ
ܒܡܕܝܢܬܐ܆
ܘܐܬ̈ܬܘ ܠܘܬ
ܘܫܡܥܘ ܫܬ
ܐܘܟ ܒ̈ܢܝܢ
ܘܡܬܐ̈ܒܠܝܢ
ܥܠ ܩ̈ܕܝܫܐ
ܕܐܬܩ̈ܛܠܘ܆
ܘܟ̈ܠܗ ܘܫܩܠܘ
ܦܓܪ̈ܝܗܘܢ
ܕܩܕ̈ܝܫܐ
f. 71b ܡܒܪ̈ܟܝܢ܆
ܘܗܘܘ
ܡܬܐ̈ܒܠܝܢ
ܘܒ̈ܟܝܢ
ܡܪܝܪܐܝܬ܆
ܣܓ̈ܝܢ
ܡܪܝܪܘܬܗ
ܕܡܫܬܢܝܐ
ܡܕܒܪܐ
ܘܫܬܩܐ

f. 46b ܪܒܐ ܕܠܡܐ ܒܠܫܘܕ f. 46b
ܒܦܓܪܗ ܡܐܢܘ،
ܒܝܫܐܝܬ ܘܦܠܓ ܘܠܦܓܪܗ
ܐܠܐ ܠܐ ܠܐ ܘܪܒ ܀
ܕܡܘܬ ܀ ܗܘܐ ܕ،
ܐܘܪܝܘܢ ܝܕܐ ܒܗ
ܕ، ܠܐ ܒܦܓܪ̈ܗܘܢ
ܗܘܐ ܒܗ ܕܘܪ̈ܝܫܝܐ
ܐܘܠܘܣ ܗܢܘ ܡܬܝܢ ܀
ܡܫܘܫ ܗܘ ܕ،
ܕܒܠܘܡ ܀ ܣܡܐ ܗ̇ܘ،
ܒܪܒܪܐ ܓܪ ܘܒܘܪ ܗܘܐ
f. 43a ܕܡܫܝܚܐ ܢܬܗ ܣܓܠ ܒܡܟ f. 43a
ܒܟܝܦܐ ܥܠ ܒܦܓܪ̈ܗܘܢ
ܒܪܘܣܗ ܕܘܪ̈ܝܫܝܐ ܀
ܡܢ ܡܫܝܚܐ ܗܘܐ ܕ،
ܠܡܫܠܡܗ ܡܚܝܘ
ܗܘܐ ܕ، ܘܡܬܐܒܠ
ܦܓܪ ܕܦܓܠ ܥܠ ܟܘܠ
ܢܬܗ ܘܠܐ ܡܢܐ ܕܦܓܠܐ
ܕ، ܐܒܪ ܠܘܪ̈ܝܫܝܐ ܀
ܢܬܗ ܒܠܘܡ ܦܪ̈ܝܫ ܕ،

f. 46a ܡܢܐ ܠܬܠܡܝ̈ܕܝ
ܥܒܝܪ: ܘܗܦܟܘ
ܡܢ ܦܬ̈ܢܝ
ܒܗܘ ܝܘܡܐ
ܬܘܡܢܝܢ
ܘܐܪ̈ܒܥܐ
ܒܒ̈ܪܝܢ :·
ܘܗܦܟ ܕ̈ܠܗܘ
ܒܡܪܒܐ :·
ܗܡܢܐ ܠܐ
ܡܢܬܘ :·
f. 43b ܗܠܝܢ ܕ̇ܝ
ܒܠܚ̈ܝܢ
ܦܐܝܐܝܬ ܡܢܗ
ܒܡܪ̈ܒܝܐ
ܠܒܪ ܒܢ̈ܝܗܘܢ
ܒܪ ܡܢܐ
ܕܐܬܗܦܟܘ
ܒܠܒܗܘܢ :·
ܘܠܐ ܐܝܬܝܪ
ܡܢܗܘܢ
ܐܘܦ ܚܕ :·

f. 46a ܐܢܐ ܕ̇ܝ
ܒܪ ܗܠܝܢ
ܡܬܒܒ̈ܪܢ
ܐܬܚܝܠܬ
ܐܢܐ ܘܢܦܫܝܬ
ܡܢ ܙܘܝܬܐ
ܕܗܘܝܬ
ܠܡܚܪ ܒܗ̇ :·
ܘܒܚܝܬ ܕ̇ܝ
ܡܫܟܚܘܪ
ܒܩܪ̈ܝܗܘܢ
f. 43b ܕܡܪ̈ܕܝܢܐ :·
ܘܐܬܚܫܒܬ
ܒܠܒܗܘܢ
ܕܐܬܗܦܟܘ
ܠܒܪ ܡܢ ܬܠܬܐ
ܕܗܡܢܘܗ
ܘܐܘܪܝܢ
ܘܐܢܙܪܝܢܗ
ܕܗܡܢܘܗ
ܕ̇ܝ ܗܘܐ
ܒܫܘܢܝܐ

ܘܫܡܫܘ f. 59b
ܒܩܛܠܐ
ܐܬܘ ܗܢܘܢ
ܦܪܕܝܐ
ܒܗܝ ܐܘܦ
ܗܢܘܢ
ܒܪ̈ܒܝ
ܠܬܕܘ
ܠܪ̈ܚܡܘܗܝ
ܠܡܪܒܐ
ܘܪ̈ܚܡܘ
ܠܪ̈ܚܡܘܗܝ f. 62a
ܡܢ ܡܒܢ̈ܐ:
ܢܚܫܕ ⁖
ܘܫܪ̈ܘ ܕܝ
ܒܡܪܒܐ
ܡܢ ܡܕܝܢܬܗ
ܕܫܡܫܐ
ܒܐܬܪ ܫܘܐ
ܘܠܪ̈ܝܪܝܐ
ܦܠܓܗܘܢ
ܒܦܠܓ

ܗܘܘ ܫܪ̈ܝܢ ⁖ f. 59b
ܦܪ̈ܝܫܝ ܕܝ
ܗܘܘ ܣܓܝ
ܡܢ ܒܪ̈ܒܝ ⁖
ܘܗܘܘ ܡܠܠܝܢ
ܒܒܪ̈ܒܝ ⁖
ܗܠܝܢ ܕܝ
ܒܪ̈ܒܝ
ܒܪ ܡܠܟܘ
ܣܒܪܐ
ܕܚܝ̈ܠܘܗܝ ⁖
ܕܠܐ ܗܘܘ f. 62a
ܡܠܝܢ ܒܪ̈ܡܫܝܢ
ܗܠܝܢ
ܕܢܫܬܘܕܘܢ ⁖
ܒܗܝ ܡܕܡ
ܒܫܘܠܛ
ܘܣܓܝ
ܣܘܒܪ̈ܘ
ܒܡܪܒܐ ⁖
ܗܘܐ ܕܝ
ܡܪܒܐ ܒܪ

f. 59a ܘܫܡܗ ܐܘܢ
ܐܠܗܐ
ܬܒܢܝܪܐ
ܘܢܒܪܗܘܢ
ܡܦܠܠ
ܘܐܬܦܠܓ
ܪܓܘܢܐ
ܕܡܒܪܗܘܢ :
ܘܗܘܘ ܕܝ
ܡܬܢܨܒܝܢ
ܕܗܡܝܢ
f. 62b ܢܬܘܒܘܢ
ܠܐܬܪܗܘܢ :
ܘܠܐ ܗܘܐ
ܡܠܝܢ ܕܐܠܗܐ
ܗܘܬ ܬܒܢܝܪܐ :
ܘܡܢ ܫܡܥܬܐ
ܕܝ ܡܦܠܠܘ
ܢܫܢܐ ܘܦܠܠܢܐ :
ܘܡܢ ܒܬܪ
ܒܢ ܫܡܥܘ
ܢܘܪܐ

f. 59a ܒܕܩܠܝܐ :
ܘܦܠܓ ܐܘܨܕܘ
ܕܩܠܝܢ ܕܠܐ
ܒܪܫܡܝܢ
ܗܡܝܢ ܕܝ
ܕܢܫܪܒܘܢ
ܐܬܪܐ :
ܘܒܕ ܗܘܢ
ܒܥܕܝܢ ܗܠܝܢ
ܐܬܘ ܐܢܫܝܢ
ܡܢ ܦܪܢ :
f. 62b ܠܒܪܝܢ
ܫܘܠܝܢ
ܥܢܬ ܡܐܟܐ
ܒܡܢܝܐܢ
ܒܫܫܪܝܢ :
ܘܒܪܒܪܢ
ܕܝ ܗܘܘ
ܡܐܓܡܝܢ
ܠܒܕܠ
ܐܬܪܗܘܢ :
ܘܒܕ ܡܓܘ

f. 22b ܕܡܫܝ̈ܚܐ ܀
ܘܗܘܘ ܒܟ̈ܝܢ
ܕܢܦ̈ܩܘܢ
ܒܝܡܐ
ܘܐܙ̈ܠܘܢ
ܠܛܠܘܪܒܐ:
ܗܝܟ ܡܐ
ܕܗܘܐ
ܢܒܝܘܗܘܢ
ܡܢ ܩܘܕܡ
ܕܐܙ̈ܠܘܢ ܀
ܘܐܙ̈ܠܘ
f. 15a ܘܐܬ̈ܟܣܘ
ܐܠܦܐ
ܬܒܝܪܐ
ܘܫܒܪܗܘܢ
ܦܠܛ ܀ ܗܘ
ܒܪ ܕܫܒ̈ܩܘ
ܕܢܦܠܘܢ ܒܬܗ
ܐܠܦܐ ܀
ܪܫܡܗ
ܕܡܫܝܚܐ

f. 22b ܗܘܐ ܀ ܘܡܛܠ
ܕܒܛܘܪܣ̈ܡ
ܢܒܪܘܫ
ܠܒܪ ܡܢ
ܒܪܒܪܝܐ
ܕܗܘܐ ܒܥܡܗ
ܒܐܠܦܐ ܀
ܘܡܛܠ ܫ̈ܠܝܚܐ
ܕܐܠܦܐ ܀
ܘܐܬܡܨܬ ܡܢ
ܚܕܐ ܠܥܢܝܐ
ܘܐܬܬܒܪܬ ܀
f. 15a ܘܡܛܠ ܠܗܘ
ܒܪܒܪܝܐ
ܕܗܘܐ ܒܥܡܗ
ܒܐܠܦܐ:
ܘܪܒܐ ܠܒܪܒܗ
ܠܝܡܐ ܀
ܘܒܫܘܫܛܗ
ܕܐܠܗܐ
ܐܫܬܘܙܒ
ܠܛܘܪܐ ܀

f. 22 a ܕܡܟܠܘܫܘܢ
ܘܡܫܒܚܝܢ
ܠܗ܀ ܘܗܘܝܬ
ܡܕܒܪܐ
ܡܢ ܒܝܢ
ܫܒ̈ܚܬܐ
ܐܚܪܬܝ
ܡܐܪ̈ܬܘܢ
ܠܘܬܝ܀
ܘܗܘܝܬ
ܕܝ ܚܙܝܐ
ܒܚܝ̈ܠܐܝ
f. 15b ܡܚܘܬܝ܀
ܘܒܬܪ ܗܘܝܬ
ܡܢ ܐܠܗܐ
ܕܐܝܟ ܗܘܐ
ܨܒܝܢܗ
ܕܬܬܦܠܛ
ܡܢܗܘܢ܀
ܘܐ̈ܬܘ ܟܕ
ܡܛܐ ܠܢܘܬܐ܀
ܘܟܕ ܕܝ

f. 22 a ܕܢܣܒܘ
ܕܗܦ̈ܟܝܢ
ܗܢܝܢ ܕܕ̈ܠܝܢ܀
ܒܦܪ̈ܘ
ܒܠܝܗܘܢ
ܘܪ̈ܢܝܢ ܡܢܝ܀
ܕܐܠܗܐ
ܟܕ ܒܣܪ
ܒܢ̈ܝܗܘܢ ܕܠܐ
ܢܣܒܘܢ ܠܗ܀
ܘܫܒܩܘ ܕܝ
ܠܗܪ̈ܫܝܐ
f. 15 b ܪ̇ܚܡܝܢ
ܦܠܓܗܘܢ
ܟܠ ܦܠܓ܀
ܘܟܕ ܕܝ
ܕܠܐ ܐܫ̈ܟܚܘ
ܟܠܗܘܢ
ܕܢܦ̈ܩܘܢ
ܬܐ̈ܒܘ
ܠܗܘܢ ܠܓܒ
ܡܒܘ̈ܥܐ

f. 1b ܫܪܝܐ
ܬܗܘܢ
ܡܪܦܝ̈ܢ
ܠܝܬ ܐܢܫܐ
ܡܫܬܒܠ ܀
ܕܠܫܘܝܢܐ
ܒܪ ܫܘܒܪ̈ܘ ܀
ܒܥܠܘܡܐ
ܕܝ ܐܒܪ̈ܝܢ
ܐܒܪ̈ܝܢ
ܐܬܦܠܓܘ ܀
ܗܝܟ ܡܪ̈ܦܠܓܝܢܐ ܀
f. 8a ܒܪ̈ܒܪܝ
ܕܝ ܗܘܘ
ܫܒܝ̈ܢ
ܕܦܬ̈ܠܘ
ܒܠܒܘܢ ܀
ܘܗܘܘ ܕܝ
ܡܚܠܬܒܝܢ
ܒܟܘܠ ܐܬܪ ܀
ܫܒܝ̈ܢ
ܕܢܚ̈ܒܫܘܢ

f. 1b ܕܗܒ ܀ ܘܠܐ
ܗܘܘ ܡܕܟ̈ܝܢ
ܕܠܝܬ ܡܪ̈ܥܝܢܐ
ܡܢܝܢ ܟܠܗܘܢ
ܟܠ ܐܪ̈ܒܥܐ ܀
ܐܢܫܐ ܕܝ ܒܗ
ܢܨܚܬ ܗܠܝܢ
ܒܟܠܗܘܢ
ܡܬܒܪ̈ܟܝ ܀
ܡܫܬܬ ܗܝ
ܕܫܠܬܐ ܀
ܘܒܘܕ ܦܓܪܐ
f. 8a ܕܐܕܘܩ ܠܐ
ܐܫܬܬܪܬ
ܒܝ ܀ ܐܠܐ
ܐܬܒܒܕܬ
ܗܝܟ ܡܫܬܐ ܀
ܒܕ ܗܘܝܬ
ܦܓܪܝ ܒܝܢ
ܥܒ̈ܕܬܐ ܀
ܕܗܘܝܬ ܐܡܪ
ܕܗܐ ܠܗܘܢ

f. 1a ܘܠܐ ܦܪ̈ܫܘ
ܡܢ ܚܒܬܗ
ܕܡܫܝܚܐ ܀
ܗܢܝܢ ܡܢܐ
ܕܟܬܝܒ ܀
ܕܡ̇ܢ ܡܦܪܫ
ܠܢ ܡܢ
ܚܒܬܗ
ܕܡܫܝܚܐ ܀
ܕܠܐ ܫܘܦ
ܘܠܐ ܠܫܘܝܢ
ܠܐ ܡܦܪ̈ܫܝܢ
f. 8b ܠܢ ܡܢ
ܚܒܬܗ
ܕܡܫܝܚܐ ܀
ܗܟܢ ܐܘܦ
ܗܠܝܢ ܡܕܒܪ̈ܝܐ
ܘܪ̈ܚܡ
ܦܓܪ̈ܝܗܘܢ
ܠܠܫܢ̈ܝܐ
ܘܠܫܦܐ ܀
ܐܢ ܐܘܢ

f. 1a ܕܡܠܟܐ
ܬܗܘܢ ܀
ܕܢܫܒܬܗܘܢ
ܗܘܬ ܕܝ
ܒܫܘܡܠܝܐ
ܠܘܬ ܡܪ̇ܐ
ܐܠܗܗܘܢ ܀
ܘܗܘܘ
ܢܐܘܣܘܢ
ܡܕܝ̈ܢܬܐ
ܠܐܠܗܐ
ܡܪܘܡܡܐ ܀
f. 8b ܘܫܪ̈ܘܘ
ܒܠܒܐ
ܒܒܘܪܐ
ܘܬܪܘܦܐ
ܘܠܐܠܗܐ
ܒܠܫܘܕ
ܕܒܫܘ ܀
ܘܗܒܕܢ
ܐܬ̈ܬܠܗܘ
ܒܫܦܐ ܀

[Right column]

f. 20 b ܥܢܝ̈ܢܝܗܘܢ
ܘܦܠܓܘ ܠܘܬܗ
ܐܒ̈ܗܝܢ ܐܒ̈ܗܝܢ ܀
ܘܗܘܐ ܚܕܐ
ܘܐܡܪ̇
ܡܒܪܟ ܗܘ
ܡܪܐ ܕܠܐ
ܐܫܠܡ
ܠܘܬܝ ܒܢܝ
ܐܚ̈ܝܗܘܢ
ܕܪ̈ܚܝܡܐ ܀
ܘܒܪ ܕܝ
f. 17 a ܐܡܪ̇ ܗܠܝܢ ܀
ܫܠܡ ܪ̇ܘܚܗ
ܒܡܪܐ ܀ ܘܡܢ
ܒܬܪ ܕܡܝܬ
ܡܢܘ ܗܘܬ
ܫܠܝ: ܘܒܪ
ܢܚܝܬ ܕܝ
ܗܠܝܢ ܗܘܝܬ
ܡܫܝܚ
ܠܐܠܗܐ

[Left column]

f. 20 b ܕܡܫܡܫܐ
ܠܘܬܝ ܡܢ
ܒܢܝܢܗܘܢ
ܕܠܐ ܢܣܒܘܢ
ܠܘܬܝ ܀ ܗܘܝܢ
ܕܢܬܦܠܓ
ܘܢܥܒܪ
ܒܦܠ̈ܚܘܗܘܢ
ܕܡܕܝ̈ܢܬܐ
ܕܐܬܬ̈ܦܠܘ
ܬܬܡ ܀ ܘܡܠܘ
ܒܥܠܡ
f. 17 a ܒܢܝܢܬܐ
ܐܕܡ ܡܢ
ܐܕܝܡܗܘܢ
ܕܡܕܝ̈ܢܬܐ
ܕܐܬܬ̈ܦܠܘ ܀
ܘܐܬܬܠܡ
ܒܟܠ ܙܒܢܘܢ
ܠܟ ܀ ܘܡܘܕܝܢ
ܗܘܘ ܠܐܠܗܐ
ܟܠ ܗܠܝܢ

f. 20a ܠܐ ܢܟܘ
ܕܢܦܩܘܢ
ܠܘܬܗ ⁘ ܐܠܐ
ܚܕ ܐܘܢ
ܡܢܗܘܢ
ܕܒܪ ܠܘܬܗ
ܠܒܪ ⁘
ܒܪ ܡܫܠܘܢ

ܘܒܪ ܕܝ
ܫܡܐ
ܐܫܘܢ ܕܠܐ
f. 17b ܐܫܬܘܝ
ܠܗ ܕܢܬܦܠܠ
ܥܡ ܗܠܝܢ
ܡܕ̈ܒܪܝܐ ⁘
ܥܡ ܐܚܪ * *
* * * *
* * * ܥܡ
ܒ̈ܢܝ ܠܗ
ܫܦܝܐ ܥܡ
ܕܗܘܐ ܕ

f. 20a ⌈ܐܢܫ⌉ ܠܗ ⁘
ܘܡܫܝܚܐ ܚܕ
⌈ܡܢܗܘܢ⌉
ܟܠ ܟܬܒܗ
ܗܠܝܢ ܕܝ
ܠܬܠܡܝܕ
ܘܢܦܩܘܢ
ܠܘܬܗ ⁘ ܗܕܐ
ܒܪ ܗܘܬ
⌈ܬ⌉ܫܡܫܬܗ
⌈ܬ⌉ܕܫܡܫܬ
ܥܡ ܗܠܝܢ
f. 17b ܡܕ̈ܒܪܝܐ ⁘
ܗܠܝܢ ܕܝ
ܕܢܬܦܠܠ⌉ ܥܡ
ܗܠܝܢ
ܡܫܡܫܢܐ
ܒܥܡ ܕܝ ܢܚܪܘ
ܟܠܗܘܝ
ܒܫܡܐ
ܘܐܕܪ̈ܟܘ ܒܗ
ܘܫ̈ܒܘ[1] ܟܠܗܘܝ

[1] Cod. ܘܫܪ̈ܘ

f. 74 b ܗܝܕܝܢ ܒ̇ܪ
ܫܡܫܓܪ̈ܡܝ
ܫܒ̈ܝܢ : ܗܕ݂ܢ
ܡܢ ܬܠܡܝܕܘܬܗ
ܐܠܦ ܝܬܗ
ܐܒܐ ܝܘܣܝܦ
ܕ݁ܒܝ̇ܪܐ
ܕܚܣܝܕܘܬܐ :
ܕܡܢ ܬܠܡܝܕܘܬܗ
ܢܣܒ ܠܗ
ܠܡܕܒ̇ܪܐ :
ܡܬܬܬܫ
f. 81 a ܠܡܘܒܠ
ܣܦܝܢܐ :
ܒܒܦܢܐ
ܘܒܗܘܬܐ :
ܗܕ݂ܢ ܐܘܢ
ܟܕ݂ ܫܡ̈ܥܘ
ܒܪ̈ܒ̈ܝ
⌈ܠ⌉ܗܘ ⌈ܬ⌉ܠܡܝܕܐ
* ⌈ܪ̈ܫܝ⌉ܫܢܐ
* * * *

f. 74 b ܟܕ݂ ܕ݁ܝܢ ܗܘܐ
ܡܬܢܐ
ܠܝ ܗܠܝܢ
ܗܘܐ ܟܒܐ
ܘܕ݁ܡܒܘܝ
ܢܦܩܬ݂ܢ ܗܝܕܝܢ
ܫܠܝܐܢ
ܕܡ̈ܢܝܢ : ܗܝܕܝܢ
ܕܐܘܦ ܐܝܢ
⌈ܡ⌉ܕ⌈ܡ⌉ܕܡܝܢ ⌈ܗܘܘܢ⌉
ܒܘ⌈ܠܝ⌉ܢ :
ܘܬܘܒܢ
f. 81 a ܗܘܐ ܐܡܪ̇
ܠܝ ܡܢܐ
ܠܐܡܘܪ̇
ܐܢܐ ܗܝܕܝܢ
ܠܬܝ ܡܢܐ
ܕܢܡܚܐ ܚܢ̈ܢܐ
* * * *
* * * *
* * * *
* * * *

f. 74 a ܒܪܘܚܬ
ܕܝ ܐܢܐ
ܘܐܬܦܠܒܪܬ
ܬܚܡܝ ܀ ܘܗܘܝܬ
ܡܬܚܫܒ.
ܕܫܪܐ ܡܢ
ܬܪ̈ܬܝܐ
ܡܬܟܒܕ
ܠܝ ܀ ܐܢ̇ܐ
ܡܬܦܝܐ
ܐܢܐ ܀ ܐܢ̇ܐ
ܡܬܦܝܫ.
f. 81 b ܐܢܐ ܘܡܬܠܠܝܢ
ܠܝ ܀ ܗܠܝܢ
ܕܝ ܙ̈ܢܝܢܝܐ
ܒܢ̈ܝܢܝ
ܥܡܘ ܬܪ̈ܝܢ
ܐܒܗ̈ܬܐ
ܕܡܬܠܠܘ
⌜ ⌝ܒܫܪܬܐ
ܘܡܠܠܝܢ
⌜ܠܡܥܢܬܐ⌝

f. 74 a ܗܝܢ ܫܪܐ ⁞
ܒܥܘܡܘܬܐ
ܡܠܠܝܢ
ܘܗܦ̈ܝܟܐ
ܒܐܪ̈ܙܝܗܘܢ
ܥܠ̈ܝܗܝܢ ܀
ܘܟܘܠ ܡܢ
ܕܗܘܘ ܦ̈ܠܚܝܢ
ܒܗ ܗܘܘ
ܡܠܠܝܢ ܕܠܐ
ܒܪ̈ܝܚܝܢ ܀
ܡܢܗܘܢ ܠܝ̇
f. 81 b ܠܩ̈ܘ ܟܠ
ܙ̈ܢܝܗܘܢ ܀
ܘܫܘܪ ܟܠ
ܟܬܒܗ ܀
ܡܢܐ ܠܝ ܕܝ
ܕܝܐܡܘܪ
ܘܣ * * *
* * * *
* * * *
* * * *

f. 81 b is not a palimpsest; but several lines are cut away.

f. 36b ܗܘܝܢ ܕܐܬܬ
ܐܡܪ ܠܝ
ܒܢ̈ܝ ܐܝܟ
ܒܒܢ̈ܝܟ ܀
ܡܢܐ ܐܦ Ps. 116. 12
ܪܘܥܐ
ܠܡܪܐ
ܚܘܠܦ ܡܢܐ
ܕܥܒܕ ܠܝ
ܒܗ ܕܡܫܝܚܘ
ܢܦܩܠ ܘܒܫܡܗ
ܕܡܪܝܐ
ܩܕܝܫܐ
f. 37a ܢܦܪܐ :
○ܒܡ ܬܠܐ
ܐܒܘܢ
ܐܣܩܘܝ
ܠܫܘܒܚܐ
ܘܐܡܪ
ܡܪܐ ܝܫܘܥ
ܡܫܝܚܐ
ܒܪܗ
ܕܐܠܗܐ

f. 36b ܢܫܝܐ ܕܠܐ
ܡܐܬ ܀ ܠܐ
ܬܬܥܢܐ
ܬܗܘܢ
ܠܒܪ̈ܝܢ ܀ ܐܠܐ
ܐܬܕܒܪ
ܠܢܘܟܪܝܢ
ܘܡܫܡܫܢܘܬܗܘܢ ܀
ܘܢܫܠ ܬܗܘܢ
ܒܗܕܐ
ܫܒܬܐ
ܕܠܫܘܢܐ
f. 37a ܗܕܝܢ : ܘܩܒܠ
ܩܘܪܒܢܐ
ܕܢܟܣܬ
ܒܪܫ.
ܒܣܝܦ
ܘܩܕܡܝܗܘܢ ܀
ܕܠܗܘܢ ܫܐܦܪ
ܐܣܦܪܐ
ܘܬܫܒܘܚܬܐ
ܠܥܠܡܝܐ

Two pages = one leaf of the ancient MS., are missing here

f. 36a ܐܬܬܣܝܡܬ
ܠܗܘܢ
ܕܒܗܘܢ
ܬܝܪ̈ܘܬܘܢ
ܚܝ̈ܐ
ܕܠܥܠܡ ܗܝܢ
ܬܫܬܘܬܦܘܢ
ܕܬܗܘܘܢ
ܒܗܘܢ
ܒܗ̇ ܚܕܘܬܐ:
ܗܕܐ ܕܡܛܝܒܐ
ܠܟܘܠ ܗܠܝܢ
f. 37b ܕܪ̈ܚܡܘ
ܠܡܪܢ ܝܫܘܥ:
ܠܒܪܗ
ܒܪܝ ܠܐ
ܬܬܒܝܢܘܢ
ܐܬܠܝܦܘ
ܕܡܫܝܚܐ
ܒܪ ܐܠܗܐ
ܚܠܦܐ: ܘܠܐ
ܡܬܦܝܣ

f. 36a ܠܗܘܢ ܘܠܐ
ܬܬܢܟܘܪ
ܢܦܫܗܘܢ
ܘܠܐ ܕܝ
ܬܬܒܥܘܢ [ ]
ܚܠܘܦ ܕܠܐ
ܫܦܝܪ ܠܟ
ܠܐܫܬܡܥܐ
ܕܠܡ: ܐܠܐ
ܠܟܘܫܘ
ܚܠܐ ܘܚܪܘ
ܘܓܒܘܪܬܐ
f. 37b ܕܡܫܒܪܘܢ [ ]
ܟܠܒ ܫܦܐ
ܘܓܝܒܪ:
ܘܐܠܗܐ
ܡܩܒܠ ܠܗܘܢ
ܒܡܠܟܘܬܗ:
ܘܚ̈ܝܘ ܒܗܠܗܘܢ
ܘܐܡܪ̈ܘ
ܐܝܟ ܐܒܘܢ
ܒܪܐܘܪܐ:

f. 29b ܒܪ̈ܝܐ
ܗܘܘ ܫܒܚܝܢ ܀
ܒܪ̈ܒܝܢ
ܕܝ ܕܗܘܘ
ܗܠܝܢ ܘܡܬܢܣܝܢ
ܒܡܪܟܐ ܀
ܘܪܕܦܘ
ܠܡܪ̈ܘܚܝܢ ܀
ܘܦܠܠܘ
ܡܢܗܘܢ
ܕܝ ܡܟܐܐ
ܘܐܪܟܒܝܢ
f. 28a ܘܫܘܒܚܐ ܀
ܘܫܒܝ̈ܚܬܐ
ܒܪܘܢ ܠܐܦܐ
ܦܘܪ̈ܝܐ ܀
ܘܡܛܘܗܘܢ
ܐܬܦܠܓܪܘ
ܒܝܢ ܐܘܠܝܢܐ ܀
ܘܡܬܒܘ
ܒܪ̈ܒܝܢ
ܡܢ ܒܬܪ

f. 29b ܕܫܠܝܐ
ܡܪܟܐ ܀ ܫܒܘ
ܠܫܪ̈ܗܘܢ
ܘܒܢ̈ܝܗܘܢ
ܘܒܘܠ ܡܐ
ܕܗܘܐ ܠܗܘܢ ܀
ܘܝܗܒܘ
ܬܗܘܢ
ܗܢ ܕܡܒܘ̈ܚܐ
ܕܡܒ̈ܝܐ ܀ ܘܡܢ
ܒܬܪ ܗܠܝܢ
ܡܫܒܫܐܬ
f. 28a ܗܢܝܢ ܚܘܫܬܐ
ܡܢ ܒܪܐ
ܪܗܛܘ
ܘܐܬܘ
ܚܠܝܢ
ܠܡܝܛܪܘܢ
ܠܗܘܢ ܕܗܘܝܢ
ܒܪܘܩܝܢ ܀ ܕܗܘܘ
ܡܚܝ̈ܬܝܢ
ܕܗܘܢ

Two pages = one leaf of the ancient MS., are missing here

[f. 29a] ܡܢ ܒܬܪ ܀
ܗܠܝܢ ܕܝ
ܒܪܒܪܝ
ܒܗ ܡܬ̈ܛܢܘ
ܣܦܪܗ
ܕܡܕܒܪܐ
ܘܒܬܪܟ
ܢܐܘ̈ܛܢܝܐ
ܕܕܒܪܘ
ܠܬܗܘܢ
ܒܬܪܘ ܬܡܢ
ܟܠ ܣܦܪܗ
[f. 28 b] ܕܡܕܒܪܐ ܟܘܠ
ܗܘ ܠܐܝܠܐ ܀
ܒܗ ܕܝ
ܕܢܦܩܬ
ܘܐܬܟܢܫ
ܠܦܪܐ
ܒܟܬܘ
ܢܐܘ̈ܛܢܝܐ
ܕܐܠܗܐ ܕܠܐ
ܡܪܘܘܢ

[f. 29a] ܒܐܠܗܐ ܀
ܘܫܒܩܘ ܚܕ
ܡܢ ܢܐܘܛܢܝܐ
ܒܐܠܗܐ
ܘܫܒܩܐ ܚܕܘ
ܠܗ ܒܢ ܚܕ
ܡܫܝܗܘܢ
ܕܠܐ ܢܫܒܩܘ
ܐܠܗܐ ܀
ܘܡܒܪܘ ܠܛܘܪܐ
ܘܐܬܘ ܚܕ
ܡܢܐ ܠܡܥ̈ܡܪܝܐ
[f. 28 b] ܕܡܕ̈ܝܢܐ ܀
◯ܐܘܪ̈ܝܫܘ
ܠܬܗܘܢ
ܦܪ̈ܘܐܝ
ܕܬܡܢ ܠܡܪܒܐ ܀
ܒܝܡ ܬܠܐ ܠܒܝܡ
ܡܥ̈ܡܪܝܐ
ܕܡܕ̈ܝܢܐ ܀
ܘܚܪ̈ܝܪܐ
ܡܢ ܬܪ̈ܝܢ

f. 65b ܒܕܚܠܐ
ܪܘܒܐ :
ܘܐܘܩ̈ܝܢܘܣ
ܓܐܦܘܣ ܥܠ
ܦܓܪܗ
ܕܡܚܐ : ܕܐܢ
ܣܡ̈ܝܬܘܢ
ܐܠܦܐ ܐܬܝܐ
ܬܘ̈ܕܒܢ
ܠܡ : ܘܒܬܪ
ܚܕ ܡܘܬ
ܐܬܚܫܒܬ
f. 70a ܐܠܦܐ ܠܦܪ
ܪܡܫܐ ܒܝܢܪܐ
ܐܬܝܐ ܠܘܬܢ :
ܫܪ̈ܩܐܝܢ
ܕܝ ܘܦܪ̈ܢܐܝܢ
ܡܟܠܝܢ ܐܘܢ
ܕܐܬ̈ܬܟܣܘ
ܬܘܡܢ ܐܬܬܟܬܕܘ
ܕܡ̈ܟܣܘܢ
ܡܪܒܐ ܒܡ

f. 65b ܒܠܡܐܝܢ :
ܠܒܙܠ
ܢܟ̈ܪܗܘܢ
ܘܒܢ̈ܝܗܘܢ :
ܘܐܬܟܒܫܘ
ܒܡܚܢܐ
ܡܐܬܝܢ
ܒܓ̈ܢܝܢ ܠܒܪ
ܡܢ ܢܟ̈ܣܐ
ܘܒܢ̈ܝܗܝܢ :
ܥܠ ܦܘܪܐ
ܕܠܒܠ ܡܢ
f. 70a ܕܩ̈ܠܐ ܗܘ
ܕܡܫ̈ܘܒܢܐ
ܕܡܢ̈ܟܐ : ܐܝܟ
ܕܝ ܒ̈ܢܘܢ
ܠܒܝܫܬܐ
ܕܝܠܢ ܕܡܒܢܢܐ
ܒܠܒܝܢ
ܘܪܘܚܗ
ܕܒܪܘܗ
ܬܠܬ ܡܘܡܝܢ

f. 65a ܣܓܕܐ ܘܣܓܕܘ
ܐܠܦܐ
ܕܗܘܬ
ܒܒܪܐ
ܡܢ ܐܠܗܬ :·
ܘܐܡܪܘ ܠܢ
ܕܒܥܘ ܡܢܟ
ܠܡܠܘܟܐ :·
ܘܠܝܬ ܐܢܫ
ܡܫܠܡ ܡܬܒܥܘܢ :·
ܘܐܡܪܝܢ
ܠܗܘܢ ܡܢ
f. 70b ܕܩܠܝܢ ܕܠܟܐ
ܡܬܩܠܘܢ
ܡܬܢ :· ܐܝܢ
ܡܥܪܝܢ
ܡܬܟܘܢ :·
ܘܗܘܝܢ
ܡܫܡܫܝܢ
ܐܡܪܬܝ
ܡܟܘܫ
ܪܘܫܐ

f. 65a ܕܕܪܘܡܐ :·
ܘܦܪܘܫ ܗܘܝܢ
ܒܝܬܘܗܘܢ :·
ܐܥܡܪܢ ܕܝ
ܒܚܝܠܗ
ܕܐܠܗܐ
ܠܠܝܐ ܗܘܝܢ
ܕܢܬܩܠܩ
ܡܢ ܒܢ
ܐܡܬܝܗܘܢ :·
ܗܘܐ· ܐܢܝ
ܐܡܪܝܢ ܠܗܘܢ
f. 70b ܐܝܕܗܘ
ܘܢܦܩܘ
ܒܪܚܡܘܢ
ܕܠܟܐ ܐܡܪܬܝ
ܡܐܬܘܢ ܠܟܐ
ܘܠܟܘܠܟܘܢ
ܡܬܦܠܘܢ :·
ܗܒܝ ܕܝ
ܫܡܥܝܢ ܗܠܝܢ
ܗܘܝܢ

f. 14b ܘܡܫܒܚܝܢ
ܐܝܬܝܢ ܝܬܗ
ܠܒܝܫܬܐ :
ܘܗܘܘ ܐܦܘ̈ܗܝ
ܡܢܗܪ̈ܝܢ
ܗܝܟ ܣܗܪܐ
ܕܢܗܘܪܐ :
ܘܫܗܪ̈ܝܢ
ܟܠܗܘܢ
ܟܘܠܗ
ܠܠܝܐ :
ܘܐܫܬܒܚܢ
f. 9a ܝܬܗ ܒܗܝ
ܡܕ̈ܫܝܢܐ
ܕܕܡܒܘ
ܬܚܬ ܒܐܬܪܐ :
ܗܠܝܢ ܕܝ
ܐܒܗ̈ܬܐ
ܡܕ̈ܫܝܢܐ ܗܘܘ
ܡܫܠܡܝܢ
ܘܡܒܐܬܪ̈ܝܢ
ܒܕܒܪܗܘܢ

f. 14b ܘܒܢ̈ܝ ܠܘܬܐ
ܘܒܫܘܠܛܢܐ
ܕܠܗܘܢ :
ܗܘܝܢ ܕܝ
ܒܐܪ̈ܒܥܝܢ
ܘܬܠܬܐ
ܒܥܣ̈ܪܝܢ ܒܗ
ܒܐܬܪܐ :
ܗܐ ܬܪ̈ܝܢ
ܐܢܫ̈ܝܢ ܐܬܘ
ܡܢ ܒܒܪܗ
ܕܡܠܟܐ
f. 9a ܘܐܡܪ̈ܘ ܠܝ :
ܕܬܐܘ ܡܠܟܐ
ܥܠ ܡܫܝܚ
ܕܕܩܠܝܢ
ܘܐܡܪܘ
ܠܝ ܢܛܪܘ
ܒܪܡܫܐ
ܕܗܐ ܦܠܓ
ܒܠܠܝܐ
ܐܬܘ ܡܢ

f. 14a ܒܝܫܬܗܘܢ
ܘܐܦ ܠܐ
ܗܘܐ ܫܒܩܐ
ܠܗ ܀ ܘܐܡܪ
ܠܗ ܐܒܘܢ ܀
ܗܢܐ
ܗܝ ܥܠܬܐ
ܕܐܬܝ ܐܬ
ܠܘܬ ܥܒܕܝܟ
ܘܡܟܪܢ ܀
ܘܐܡܪ
ܠܗ ܫܒܩܐ
f. 9b ܕܘܡܟܪܢ ܐܢܐ
ܐܙܠ ܠܘܬ
ܡܪܐ ܀
ܘܐܬܝܬ
ܠܘܬܟ
ܕܬܣܥܘܪ
ܦܓܪܝ ܀
ܘܗܝܟ ܕܐܬ
ܟܠܐ ܡܒܘܪ
ܫܬܗ ܀ ܘܗܦܟ

f. 14a ܡܛܠ ܗܕܐ
ܠܐܣܘܢ ܟܠ
ܟܠ ܐܣܘܬܐ
ܕܢܦܫܗ : ܘܒܗ
ܒܫܒܬܐ
ܦܫܛ ܗܕܐ
ܐܝ̈ܕܘܝ
ܠܫܘܡܝܐ
ܘܢܠܦ ܘܕܡܟ
ܒܫܠܡ ܀
◯ܪܘܚܗ ܕܝ
ܐܣܘܢ ܒܗ
f. 9b ܒܫܒܬܐ ܗܘ
ܬܠܡܝܕܗ :
ܘܒܝܙ
ܐܒܗ̈ܬܐ
ܡܕ̈ܒܪܢܐ ܀
ܘܢܣܒܢ
ܫܘ̈ܦܢܢ
ܕܕܩ̈ܠܢ
ܘܐܝܠܢ
ܘܒܬܫܒܚܬܐ

f. 26 b ܒܥܠܟ ⁘ ܘܐܡܪ
ܠܗ ܦܣܩܐ
ܣܐܘܬ
ܒܒܕܬ ܒܪܝ ⁘
ܕܘܡܣܐܝ
ܡܬܒܒܝܐ
ܓܠܘܬܐ ⁘
ܦܠܓ ܓܪ
ܗܢܝ
ܡܓܪ̈ܬܗ
ܕܒܥܠܕܒܒܐ ⁘
ܘܐܡܪ ܠܗ
f. 31 a ܬܠܡܝܕܗ
ܡܢܐ ܗܘܐ
ܠܟ ܐܒܐ
ܕܦܪܫܬ ܡܢ *⌜ܠܟ⌝
ܘܫܒܩܬ
ܠܝ ܠܚܘܕܝ ⁘
ܘܗܘܝܬ
ܡܓܝܢ ܦܠܓ ⁘
○ܘܐܡܪ ܠܗ
ܦܣܩܐ ⁘ ܒܠܬܗ

f. 26 b ܐܘܦ ܕܠܐ
ܐܬܚܫܒܬ
ܠܟ ܐܠܗܐ
ܗܘ ܕܝܕܥ ⁘
⌜ܒܪ̇ܦ⌝ ܕܝ ܒܕ
ܡܐ ܠܗܕܐ
ܫܒܬܐ ܠܐ
ܪܚܡܝܬ
ܡܢ ܗܕܢ
ܐܬܪܐ ⁘ ܘܠܐ
ܒܒܪܝܬ
ܫܕ ܒܫܘܒ ܕܠܐ
f. 31 a ܐܫܬܬܦܬ
ܒܡܒܘܢ
ܒܪ̈ܝܐ
ܡܫ̈ܝܚܐ
ܕܡܫܝܚܐ ⁘
ܘܬܡܗ
ܐܣܘܡ
ܒܣ̈ܒܬܗ
ܕܗܝܟ ܗܘܐ
ܟܠܠ ܘܢܩܡ

f. 26 a ܠܐ ܐܬܚܫܒܬ
ܠܐܚܝ ܠܒܪܝܠ
ܬܬܒܫܬܗܘܢ
ܕܒܠܢ ܢܒܐ ܀
ܐܬܬܐ ܕ̈ܝ
ܬܠܡܝܕܗ
ܕܡܫܝܚܗ
ܢܩܡܘܣ ܀
ܘܠܐ ܐܫܟܚ
ܠܡܒܐ ܀
ܘܒܟܐ ܥܠܘܗ
ܘܠܐ ܐܫܟܚ
f. 31 b ܥܠܘܗ ܀ ܘܒܟܡ
ܒܬܪ ܟܡ ܗ
ܒܡܠܬܗ
ܕܡܒܐ ܀
ܘܗܘܐ
ܡܢܝܢ ܫܢܝܢ
ܠܒܪ ܠܗ ܀
ܦܝܪ ܡܟܠܘܢ
ܡܢ ܒܬܪ ܕ̈ܝ

f. 26a ܫܢܬ ܥܠܝܡ
ܒܠܝܠܗ
ܕܝܘܡܐ
ܐܘܪ ܐܚܝ
ܟܠ ܬܪܥܐ ܀
ܘܢܦܩ ܐܫܘܢ
ܘܫܡܥܐ
ܠܡܒܐ
ܐܒܘܢ ܕܠܗ
ܡܐܡܪ ܀ ܘܡܢ̈
ܒܬܗ ܬܫܒܘܚܬܐ
ܘܗܘܐ
f. 31 b ܡܟܝܪ
ܕܪܘܚ ܗܘ ܀
ܘܒܐܬܘܬܢ
ܐܡܪ ܠܗ
ܡܠ ܐܒܐ
ܘܒܪ ܡܠ
ܘܟܠ ܒܬܗ
ܒܫܪܘܐ ܀
ܘܫܐܠ
ܦܠܝܡܘܢ

f. 53 b ܗܘܐ ܒܢ̈ܝܐ
ܒܡܫܝܚܘܬܐ
ܘܠܐ ܐܬܪܦܝ ܒܗ :
ܘܡܢ ܒܬܪ
ܣܓܝ̈ܐܐ
ܫܢ̈ܝܢ ܦܬܫ
ܬܪܥܐ
ܘܐܟܠ ܠܗ̇
ܘܒܪ ܝܠܕ̈ܝܢ
ܡܬܚ̈ܝܢ ܠܗ :
ܘܒܢܝܐ ܫܒܝܐ
ܘܐܡܪ ܠܗ:
f. 52 a ܐܡܪܬܝ
ܐܬܝ ܐܬܐ
ܠܒܐ : ܘܐܡܪ
ܠܗ ܐܫܘܥ
ܐܬܐ ܠܗ
ܐܪ̈ܒܥ ܫܢ̈ܝܢ
ܘܡܒܬܪ ܡܢ
ܕܐܬܬܝ
ܠܒܐ : ܐܠܗܐ
ܠܒܪܠ

f. 53 b ܕܠܐ ܡܠܪܦ
ܡܪܝܫܘܬܗ̇
ܠܐ ܐܘܫܛܬ :
ܘܢܦܠ ܫܒܝܐ
ܕܢܫܒܐ
ܐܫܘܥ
ܡܫܝܚܘܬܐ :
ܘܠܐ ܐܡܪ
ܠܗ ܟܠܘܡ
ܠܒܪܠ ܗܕܐ :
ܐܠܐ ܦܘܠ
ܡܐ ܕܐܫܠ
f. 52 a ܠܬܗ ܐܡܪ
ܠܗ: ܘܐܫܛ
ܫܦ̈ܝܬܐ
ܘܦܢܐ ܠܘܬܗ
ܒܫܠܡ:
ܘܡܢ ܒܬܪ
ܒܪ ܐܘܦ
ܫܒܐ ܦܢ
ܡܢ ܐܬܪܐ
ܠܘܬܗ : ܘܒܘܕ

f. 53a ܕܩܘܣܛܠܐ :
ܘܗܘܐ
ܠܗ ܚܕ
ܬܠܡܝܕ : ܠܐ
ܕܝܢ ܗܘܐ
ܒܥܡܝܪ
ܒܥܡܗ : ܐܠܐ
ܩܪܝܒ ܠܗ :
ܐܬܐ ܕܝܢ
ܚܕ ܡܢ
ܐܚ̈ܐ ܕܡܫܘܠ
ܡܘܬܗ ܥܠ ܛܒ
f. 52b ܫܡ̈ܥܬܗ :
ܘܐܡܪ ܥܠ
ܬܪܥܐ :
ܗܢܐ ܕܝܢ
ܗܘܐ ܒܢܝܐ
ܒܡܫܝܚܘܬܐ
ܕܠܘܬ
ܐܠܗܐ :
ܘܐܕܝܫ
ܐܝܣܘܦ

f. 53a ܡܢ ܬܪܥܐ
ܘܫܟܢܐ
ܠܗܦܟܐ
ܕܐܬܥܒܕ
ܥܠܘܗܝ
ܕܢܘܪ ܡܢ
ܪܫܗ ܥܕ
ܡܢܐ ܠܪ̈ܓܠܘܗܝ :
ܘܐܡܪ
ܐܝܟ
ܕܝܕܥܬ ܕܝܠܝ
ܐܬܬܘܬܬܐ :
f. 52b ܘܐܬܥܒܕܬ
ܗܝܢ ܡܢܗܬܐ :
ܘܕܟܠܝܬ ܥܠ
ܐܪܥܐ ܗܝܢ
ܫܪܐ ܥܒܕܐ :
ܘܬܘܒ
ܡܢܚܬ
ܘܢܬܒܬ
ܗܝ ܕܬܪܥܐ :
ܗܦܟܐ ܕܝ

f. 42b ܒܝܘܡ ܫܪܝܘܬ
ܐܟܡܗܬܐ
ܘܕܡܫܢܐ
ܐܬܩܛܠܘ :
ܐܝܟ ܐܘܢ
ܠܟܘܠ ܚܕ
ܡܢܗܘܢ
ܡܬܕܒܪ :
ܕܒܪܝܢ
ܡܢ ܗܠܝܢ
ܐܝܟ ܡܫܠܡ :
ܕܐܬܡܘܪ
f. 47a ܡܟܐ ܕܒܟܪܘ
ܘܐܘܕܥܘ
ܕܒܝܪܐ
ܕܐܬܠܒܫܬܗܘܢ :
ܟܠ ܚܕ ܕܝ
ܚܕ ܡܢܗܘܢ
ܐܝܟ ܡܬܕܒܪ
ܕܒܝܪܗ
ܕܐܟܐ
ܘܣܦܩ

f. 42b ܕܗܘܐ ܡܢ
ܐܝܠܬ :
ܕܗܘܐ
ܒܡܢܝܢ ܠܒܪ
ܡܕܝܢܬܐ
ܟܠ ܬܪܝܢ
ܡܠܝܢ : ܪܚܡ
ܕܝ ܡܢ ܡܢܝܢܐ :
ܘܒܢܝܐ ܠܗ
ܩܠܝܐ ܗܘ
ܒܐܝܕܘܝ :
ܘܗܘܐ
f. 47a ܡܫܠܡ
ܒܢܝܫܗ
ܕܐܠܗܐ :
ܘܒܚܝܪ ܒܗ
ܒܩܠܝܬܐ
ܬܠܬܝܢ ܫܢܝܢ :
ܘܗܘܐ ܒܗ
ܕܐܦܝܣܩܘܦܘܬܐ
ܦܠܓ : ܘܕܘܒܠܝܢ
ܒܡܠܬܐ

f. 42 a ܥܠ ܛܒܗ ܕܐܒܐ ܣܝܣܘܝܣ ܡܨܪܝܐ ܀

ܗܕܢ ܕܝ ܐܒܐ ܣܝܣܘܐܝܣ ܗܘܐ ܒܥܡܪܐ ܬܡܢ ܒܫܝܗܐ ܠܟܠ ܡܢ ܐܒܐ ܗܘܫܥ ܀ ܘܒܥܡܪ ܬܡܢ ܐܪ̈ܒܥܝܢ f. 47 b ܫܢ̈ܝܢ ܘܠܐ ܕܝ ܫܠܦ ܡܢ ܠܘܬܗ ܀ ܗܕܢ ܕܝ ܡܟܢܗ ܐܬܠܒܫ ܒܩܘܢܐ ܕܐܒܐ ܗܘܝ ܛܒܒܐ ܘܫܬܡܥܐ ܀ ܗܘܐ ܕܝ

f. 42 a ܡܢܝ ܥܘܠ ܡܟܐ ܕܫܡܥܬ ܘܠܦ ܡܢ ܗܟܢܐ ܀ ܐܘܦ ܐܢܐ ܕܝ ܒܥܡܪܝܬ ܒܥܡܗ ܢܝܫܘܫ ܡܢ ܫܪܘܝܐ ܀ ܘܠܒܫܠ ܡܫܘܚܬܐ ܕܕܒܪܗ ܐܬܚܝܒܬ f. 47 b ܕܡܫܘܦ ܡܢ ܟܒܗ ܀ ܕܠܐ ܡܠܝܬ ܕܛܠܘܡܢ ܀ ܕܒܝܪܐ ܕܡܫܘܚܬܗ ܀ ܘܫܘܚܠܦܐ ܕܦܘܠܚܢܐ ܠܘܬܗ ܀ ܗܕܢ ܕܐܘܦ

f. 13b ܘܡܠܝܬ ܐܘܦ.
ܠܐ ܚܙܐ ܠܥܝܢܐ
ܘܟܘܪܐ
ܕܡܟܠܠ
ܠܗܕܐ ܓܝܪ
ܡܟܒܘܬܐ
ܡܢ ܬܫܡܫܬܗ :
ܘܒܗ ܒܫܡܫܬܐ
ܢܦܫ ܡܢܗ
ܥܝܢܐ
ܘܐܬܐܡܪ :
ܐܪܡܢܝ ܕܝ
f. 10a ܗܘܐ ܒܝܕ ܒܢܘ
ܕܠܐ ܢܫܒ
ܡܢܟܘܡܢܝܬܐ
ܘܡܫܒܬܐ :
ܒܗܠܘܢ
ܟܕ ܦܪ̈ܝܫ
ܐܪ̈ܡܢܝܐ
ܗܘܘ ܡܢ
ܘܕܘܟ :
ܘܬܒ ܠܡܕܝܢܬܗ

f. 13b ܫܠܝܡ :
ܘܗܘܐ
ܡܘܕܐ
ܠܐܠܗܐ
ܗܘ ܘܗܠܝܢ
ܕܒܥܒܗ :
ܒܒܥܗ ܕܝ
ܕܐܠܗܐ
ܠܐ ܦܬܚ
ܬܪܥܐ
ܕܥܠܝܬܗ :
ܘܠܐ ܚܣܢܐ
f. 10a ܠܐܢܫ
ܒܢܗܘܢ :

ܫܠܡ ܟܬܒܐ ܕܐܡܝܪ
ܐܟܢܐ ܣܗ̈ܕܘܗܝ
ܥܠ ܦܠܓܗ ܕܐܟܢܐ
ܡܘܫܐ

f. 13a ܒܠܚܘܕ ⁘
ܘܒܗܘܢ ܕܝ
ܘܡ̈ܫܝܚܐ
ܕܝܘܡ̈ܫܝܚܐ
ܐܬܬܘ ܠܗ
ܐܝܟ ܕܗܘܐ
ܡܬܢܣܐ ܡܢ
ܪܘܚ ܒܝܫܐ ⁘
ܗܕܝܢ ܕܝ
ܗܘܐ ܪܫܝܗ
ܕܦܪܢ ⁘ ܘܟܕ
ܕܝ ܡܬܦܠܘ
f. 10b ܠܛܘܪܐ
ܕܗܘܬ ܒܗ
ܡܥܪܬܐ
ܕܡܫܝܚܐ
ܚܙܝ ܝܬܗ
ܪܘܚܐ ܒܝܫܐ ⁘
ܘܐܠܠ ܒܥܠ
ܪܒ ܘܐܡܪ
ܐܘ ܒܝܫܐ ⁘
ܗܕܢ ܠܐ

f. 13a ܕܐܠܘܪܣ
ܒܫܡܪܐ
ܗܘܐ ܡܫܠܡ ⁘
ܒܡ̈ܫܝܚܐ ܕܝ
ܕܝܘܡ̈ܫܝܚܐ
ܕܐܪܒܥܬܐ
ܠܐ ܗܘܐ
ܦܬܚ ܬܪܥܐ
ܕܡܥܪܬܐ
ܟܕ ܡܛܐ
ܠܫܡܫܝܬܐ
ܕܫܘܒܬܐ
f. 10b ܘܫܡܫܬܐ ⁘
ܒܡ̈ܫܝܚܐ
ܕܝܘܡ̈ܫܝܚܐ
ܐܡܪ ܠܢ
ܕܡܫܡܫܝܢ
ܠܗ ܒܡܫܡ̈ܫܝܢ
ܬܘܡ̈ܫܝܢ
ܗܠܝܢ ܕܒܡܕܒܗ
ܘܫܕ ܡܣܦܠܐ
ܕܡܚܝܢ

f. 4b ܡܢ̈ܝܢ :
ܕܝܢ ܒܝܢ
ܘܗܘ̈ܝܢ ܠܢ :
ܘܗܘܝܢ ܕܝ
ܗܘܝܢ ܠܗܘܢ
ܬܘܗ̈ܝܢ
ܣܘܠܦ ܫ̈ܠܝܐ :
ܡܢ ܡܐ
ܕܗܘܝܢ
ܡܒ̈ܢܝܢ ܡܢ
ܐܬܪܐ :
f. 5a ܘܗܘܝܢ ܕܝ
ܒܒ̈ܝܢ ܝܘܪܝܢ :
ܡܢܒܘܠܬܗ
ܕܝ ܕܗܕܢ
ܘܕܝܫܐ
ܝܡܒܣܕ
ܬܘܗ̈ܝܢ
ܘܚ̈ܝܢ ܒܠܣܘܕ :
ܣܒܪ ܕܝ
ܐܘܦ ܠܐ
ܗܘܐ ܠܒܝܫ

f. 4b ܘܠܒܘܫܗ
ܕܝ ܗܘܐ
ܣܒ ܡܢ
ܕܩ̈ܠܝܐ : ܘܦܠܝ
ܗܘܐ ܪܫܡ
ܫܕܝܒܘܬܐ
ܝܬܪ ܡܢ
ܟܘܠ ܒ̈ܢܝܫܐ :
ܘܡܩܒܠ
ܗܘܐ ܒܣܕܘܐ
ܠܗܠܝܢ
f. 5a ܕܐܬ̈ܝܢ
ܠܘܬܗ
ܕܝܗܘܢ
ܫܐܠܝܢ
ܠܗ ܟܠ ܛܒ
ܫܒܬܗܘܢ :
ܡܪܕܡܒܗ
ܕܝ ܗܘܐ
ܒܬܪ ܡܘܢܐ
ܕܠܠܝܐ
ܘܫܪܝܬ

f. 4a ܒܪܘܫܡܗ
ܕܐܠܗܐ
ܐܒܐ ܡܘܫܐ
ܠܒܪ ܀ ܘܗܘܘ
ܡܗܝܡܢܝܢ
ܒܐܒܐ ܘܒܒܪܐ
ܘܒܪܘܚܐ
ܕܩܘܕܫܐ ܀
ܘܡܥܡܕܝܢ
ܕܢܫܒܘܢ
ܡܢ ܟܘܡܪܘܬܐ
f. 5b ܡܛܥܝܘܬܐ ܀
ܘܗܘܝܢ ܕܝ
ܕܡܛܝܢ
ܐܡܪܝܢ
ܥܠ ܦܓܪܗ
ܕܥܒܕܗ
ܕܐܠܗܐ
ܐܒܐ ܡܘܫܐ ܀
ܕܠܥܠܡ
ܐܝܟ ܡܢ
ܒܫܘܒܚܗ

f. 4a ܘܡܢ ܕܘ̈ܟܝܬܐ
ܒܢ̈ܬܐ
ܒܫܘܦܪܗ
ܕܡܪܢ ܝܫܘܥ
ܡܫܝܚܐ ܀
ܗܕܢ ܕܝ
ܦܪܝܫܐ
ܡܢ ܕܢܫܒ
ܐܫܬܒܫܒܐ
ܕܡܫܝܚܐ ܀
ܠܫܡ ܠܐ
f. 5b ܐܒܠ ܐܠܐ
ܬܘܡܪ̈ܝܢ
ܒܠܫܘܕ
ܗܘܐ ܐܒܠ ܀
ܐܢܫܝܢ ܕܝ
ܦܪܘܐܢܝܢ
ܕܗܘܘ
ܒܡܕܒܪܝܢ
ܬܡܢ ܀ ܗܘܘ
ܡܢܬܝܢ
ܣܓܝܢ ܡܢ

f. 73a ܕܒܫܘܠܛܢܐ
ܕܗܘܐ ܫܐܠ
ܡܢ ܐܠܗܐ
ܗܘܐ ܥܒܕ
ܠܗ: ܫܘܠܛܢܐ
ܥܠ ܦܠܓ
ܗܘܐ ܐܠܗܐ
ܥܒܕ ܒܬܪܥܗ:
ܐܬܗܡܟܬ
ܠܗ ܥܪ
ܫܘܦܠܦܘ ܟܠ
ܪ̈ܘܚܢܐ
ܟܢܫܬܐ
ܘܠ * *
* * * *
* * * *
* * * *
* * * *
* * * *
* * * *
* * * *
* * * *

f. 73a ܬܟܡ ܒܗ
ܡܕܒܪܢܐ:
ܘܐܘܦ ܠܒܢܝ̈
ܐܬܪܐ
ܦ̈ܪܢܣܝ:
ܘܒܒܕ
ܬܗܘܢ
ܒ̈ܪܫܦܝܢ:
ܐܪܓܢܝܢ
ܥ̈ܪ ܗܘܘ:
ܒܕܘ ܕܝ
ܒ̈ܪܫܦܢܝܢ:
⌜ ⌝ ܥ̈ܬܝܢ ܗܘܢ:
* * * *
* * * *
* * * *
* * * *
* * * *
* * * *
* * * *
* * * *
* * * *

f. 73 b
ܕܢܦܩܘ
ܟܠܗܘܢ :
ܠܝܬ ܐܢܐ
ܡܠ ܕܝ
ܕܝܐܡܘܪ
ܫܒܝܒܘ :
ܒܪܢ ܕܝ ܟܠ
ܫܪ ܐܐ ܬܪ̈ܝܢ
ܐܢܐ ܐܡܪܬ
ܘܗܐܦܣ
ܠܐܣܦܘܬܐ
ܕܦܘܓܠܐ
ܕܗܠܝܢ
* * * *
* * * *
* * * *
* * * *
* * * *
* * * *
* * * *
* * * *
* * * *

f. 73 b
ܠܚܠܘܬܗ
ܐܬܒܥܕ
ܠܕܒܪܐ
ܕܝܫܝܡܘܬܐ :
ܘܒܥܕ
ܒܕܒܪܐ
ܕܝܫܝܡܘܬܐ
ܥܘܒܕܝܢ
ܘܬܠܬ ܥܣܝܢ :
ܒܗ ܒܦܘܪܐ
ܕܢܦܫܢ ܡܟܢܗ
ܡܟܘܒܢ̈ܐ
ܕܡܢ̈ܝܐ :
ܐ * *
* * * *
* * * *
* * * *
* * * *
* * * *
* * * *
* * * *
* * * *

Half a leaf has been here torn away.

f. 44b ܕܡܫܝܚܗ ܢܦܫܝܢ
ܬܪܝܡܣܪܬܝ
ܬܫ̈ܒܘܚܐ
ܕܫ̈ܒܚܐ: ܗܠܝܢ
ܘܐܚܪ̈ܢ
ܟܠܗܘܢ
ܕܡܫܒܪ̈ܢ
ܘܡܩܒܠܢܐ
ܒܢܝܗܘܢ
ܒܐܪ̈ܝܢ
ܚܘܪܝܢ
ܗܢܘܢ ܢܦܫܝܢ
f. 45a ܡܢ ܩܘܪܐ
ܘܡܬܟܫܝܢ
ܗܦܟ ܕܩ̈ܠܝܢ:
ܘܒܗ ܒܩܘܪܐ
ܗܢܘܢ ܗܦܟ
ܕܡܫܬܢܝܢ
ܒܡܕܝܢ:
ܘܐܝܬ ܗܘ
ܕ̇ܝ ܒܝܬ
ܒܘܫܐ

f. 44b ܬܘܣܦܬ ܩܘܪܐ:
ܘܩܪܒ ܠܗ
ܠܩܘܪܐ
ܒܝܢܬ ܡܢ
ܫܘܬܦ
ܕܫܘܡܠܝܢ ܗܠܝܢ
ܕܒܡܪ̈ܝܢ
ܥܠ ܐܪܒܥܐ
ܘܢܦܫܬܗܘܢ
ܒܫܘܡܠܝܐ:
ܥܠ ܕܒܪ̈ܝܐ
ܕܠܗܘܢ
f. 45a ܠܝܬ ܐܢܐ
ܘܥܠ ܕܐܝܟܢܐ
ܠܐ ܓܙܪ ܚܕ
ܕܒܢ̈ܝ ܗܘܐ
ܢܕܝܢ ܐܐ
ܥܠ ܐܓܘܢܐ
ܕܐܬܥܒܕ
ܐܢܐ ܥܠ
ܢܦܫܗܘܢ
ܕܡܢ ܒܥܠܕܒܒܐ:

f. 44 a ܦܓܪܗ ܀
ܐܠܐ ܗܟܢ
ܒܦܓܪܢ ܚܫܝܢ
ܘܡܩܒܠܐ
ܕܐܬܝܬ ܠܒ.
ܬܩܝܡ ܀ ܐܬܝܬ
ܕܝ ܫܘܪܝܢ
ܕܒܡܪܘ ܬܡܢ
ܡܢ ܐܪܒܥܝܢ
ܫܢܝܢ ܘܡܢ
ܫܡܥܝܢ ܘܡܢ
ܐܡܫܬܝܢ ܀ ܘܡܢ
f. 45 b ܫܘܬ̈ܦܝܢ ܫܢܝܢ ܀
ܕܒܡܪܘ ܒܗ
ܒܐܬܪܐ ܀
ܐܝܬ ܗܘ
ܓܪ ܐܬܪܐ
ܫܘܐ ܘܡܫܝܪܐ
ܐܪܝܟܐ
ܐܪ̈ܒܥܝܢ
ܡܝܠܝܢ
ܦܬܝܗ

f. 44 a ܕܝ ܗܟܢ
ܬܪܥܣܪ
ܡܝܠܝܢ ܀
ܠܓܒܐ ܕܝ
ܡܕܢܚܐ
ܠܛܘ̈ܪܝܢ ܡܫܝܢ
ܗܟܢ ܫܘܪܐ
ܠܗܠܝܢ ܕܠܐ
ܡܒܪܝܢ ܐܬܪܐ
ܕܠܐ ܚܠܠܐ ܀
ܐܘܪܚܐ
ܡܬܒܒܪ ܬܡܢ ܀
f. 45 b ܠܡܕܒܪܐ
ܕܝ ܣܝܢܐ
ܦܣܘܩܐ
ܕܡܛܠܐ ܗܟܢ
ܕܐܡܪܝܢ
ܐܢܫܝܢ ܒܕܡܐ
ܠܐܘܣܝܘܣ
ܡܢܐ ܀ ܟܠ
ܦܣܪܗ
ܕܝ ܛܘܪܐ

f. 19b ܘܐܡܪܬ ܠܝ
ܗܕܐ ܟܠܦܘܪܐ
ܕܗܘܝܐ
ܐܝܟ ܕܒܐ
ܕܡܟܣܘܪ :
ܠܟܠ ܕܝܢܒ
ܡܕܒܪܐ
ܕܗܘܝܬ
ܚܡܝܪ ܒܗ
ܡܢ ܒܪ̈ܒܪܝ :
ܘܒܗ ܐܘܦ
ܕܢܡܒ ܐܒܐ
f. 18a ܕܘܠܘܣ
ܡܕܒܪܢܗ
ܕܐܬܪܐ
ܡܟܠ ܝܬܗ
ܒܣܕܘܐ :
ܘܗܘܐ ܫܐܠ
ܠܗ ܕܗܘܕܒ
ܠܗ ܡܘܫܦܐ
ܡܟܐ ܐܬܟܒܕ
ܠܡܕܝܢ̈ܐ

f. 19b ܕܐܬܘܦܠܘ
ܒܪܝܬܘ :
ܘܗܘܝ
ܐܬܦܠܛ ܡܢ
ܒܪ̈ܒܪܝ :
ܘܡܐ ܗܘܬ
ܦܘܠܛܝܐ
ܕܠܗܘܢ :
ܘܐܘܦ ܟܠ
ܕܒܢܝܐ
ܕܠܗܘܢ :
ܪܝܫ ܡܦܠܘܢ :
f. 18a ܘܒܗ ܐܘܦ
ܐܬܕܒܪ
ܕܒܢܝܐ
ܕܡܕܝ̈ܢܬܐ :
ܫܪܝ ܟܒܐ
ܦܠܓ ܘܐܡܪ
ܕܐܢܐ ܠܝܬ
ܠܝ ܚܡܝܪ
ܬܡܢ ܦܠܓ

f. 19a ܒܡܒܘܥܢܐ :
ܫܘ̈ܒܚܝܢ
ܕܩ̈ܠܝܢ
ܘܬܪ̈ܝܢܥܣܪ
ܡܒ̈ܢܝܢܐ
ܕܡܢܬܪܘ
⌜ܗܘ̈ܢ⌝ ܠܒ
ܗܘܢ ܡܬܢܐ :
ܗܘ ܕ̈ܝ
ܦܪܘܢܐ
ܡܬܝܢ ܠܝ ܒܠ
ܠܒ ܡܠܠܝܢܐ
f. 18b ܕܪ̈ܝܬܘ :
ܫܐܠܝܢ ܡܬܗ
ܕܝܐܡܪܘ ܠܝ
ܒܡܕ̈ܝ ܛܘܦ
ܐܬܘܦܠܠܘ :
ܘܒܡܐ ܗܘܢ ܛ
ܕܐܬܘܦܠܠܘ :
ܘܐܡܪ̇ ܠܝ
ܠܝܬ ܐܢܐ

f. 19a ܡܕ̈ܥ ܐܢܐ :
ܡܫܡܘܥ ⌜ܕ̈ܝ⌝
⌜ܫ⌝ܡܥܢܬ ܡܢ
ܚܘܪ̇ܝܢ :
ܡܢ ܗܠܝܢ
ܕܒܡܢ̈ܝܢ ܬܠ̇ܬܝܢ :
ܕܐܬܩܛܠܘ
ܒܗܠܛܘܢ :
ܛܒ ܗܘ
ܡܬܢܐ
ܠܝ : ܐܬܘ
ܚܘ̈ܪܝܢ
f. 18b ܐܒ̈ܗܬܘ
ܕܡܫܠܡܐܝܬ
ܐܬܒܒܕܬ :
ܘܒܡ ܒܬܪ̇
ܝܒܫܫ
ܘܩ̈ܡܝܢ
ܐܬܐ ܠܘܬ
ܫܒ ܫܫܫܝ
ܡܢ ܫܢ̈ܝܐ
ܕܒܡܢ̈ܝܢ ܬܠ̇ܬܝܢ

f. 76b ܡܣܡܪ ܕܝ
ܪܘܚܗ
ܠܐܠܗܐ
ܒܝܘܡܐ
ܪܒܝܥܐ ܒܬܪ
ܒܠܗܘܢ
ܡܙܝܥܐ ⁛
ܘܗܘܝܢ ܕܝ
ܕܐܝܟ ܒܐܟܠܐ
ܘܒܕܡܒܚܐ
ܐܬܐ ܚܕ
ܦܪܘܣܐܝ
f. 79a ܘܐܡܪ ܠܝ ⁛
ܕܣܝܢܝܐ
ܒܬܪ ܕܗܘܘ
ܒܡܝܪܝܢ
ܒܪܒܪܝܢ
ܠܗܘ ܐܬܪ
ܕܡܬܘܪܐ
ܪܚܬܘ
ܐܙܠܘ ܠܗܘܢ
ܘܐܬܦܠܓܘ

f. 76b ܡܢ ܒܪܒܪܝܢ ⁛
ܪܘܚܐ
ܕܝ ܗܘܬ
ܒܘܡܪܬܐ ܡܢ
ܡܗܠܟܝܢ ܬܪܝܢ
ܘܬܫܝܢ ⁛
ܗܕܐ ܕܗܝ
ܟܠ ܦܓܪܗ
ܕܝܡܐ
ܦܡܘܡܐ
ܗܢ ܕܚܪܐ
ܡܘܬܐ
f. 79a ܘܡܘܗܠܗ
ܕܐܠܗܐ
ܒܕ ܢܦܩ
ܡܢ ܡܝܪܝܢ ⁛
ܬܚܡ ܗܘܘܢ
ܬܪܝܡܣܪ
ܡܒܘܚܢܐ
ܕܡܝܢܐ
ܘܕܩܠܝܢ
ܕܒܬܝܒ

f. 76a ܕܟܢܫ. ܠܟܣܪ̈ܝ
ܥܒ̈ܕܝ ܐܬܦܣܠ :
ܗܕ. ܝ ܕܝܬܒܐ
ܗܠܟ̈ܝܢܐ
ܕܡܠܦܘܬܐ
ܘܠܐ ܒܠ ܠܗ̇ :
ܘܗܘܐ ܐܡܪ
ܒܒܘܒܐ
ܘܒܟܐ ܗܡ
ܐܠܗܐ
ܘܐܡܪ
ܐܬ ܗܘ
f. 79b ܒܠܚܘܕܝܢ
ܕܪܚܡ
ܒܢܝܫܐ :
ܠܐ ܬܫܦܪ.
ܫܬ ܗܡ
ܐܒܗ̈ܬܐ
ܡܕܫܟ̈ܢܐ :
ܗܠܝܢ
ܕܐܬܦܠܠܘ
⌜ ⌝ ⌜⌝ ܒܥܕܢܝܢ :

f. 76a ܐܠܐ ܒܝ
ܡܬܒܠܐ
ܒܚܝܝܐ
ܘܐܪܒܥܝܢܬܐ
ܒܪܦܬ̈ܝܐ :
ܐܝܟ ܒܢܪܐ
ܗܘܘ ܒܢܘܪܗ
ܕܐܠܗܐ
ܚܝܐ : ܐܬܪܚܡ
ܒܠܐܝ : ܠܒܪܢܫ
ܕܐܬ ܢܕܒ.
ܕܗܡ ܠܦܠܘܬܝ
f. 79b ܠܝܢ ܕܒܘܥܬ
ܘܠܝܢ ܐܫܒܥܬ :
ܘܠܝܢ ܕܝ
ܐܬܚܫܒܬ
ܐܢܐ ܗܒܠܐ
ܘܡܣܟܢܐ :
ܘܒܪ ܐܢܫ
ܗܠܝܢ ܒܫܥܒܕܐ
⌜ ⌝ ܫܒܝܥܐ
⌜⌝ ܘܥܪܝܪܐ

f. 55 b ܠܐ ܓܪ
ܡܠܐ ܡܠܠܬܐ
ܕܬܘܬܢܪܐ :
ܟܘܠ ܡܟܐ
ܕܢܦܫܟܝ
ܚܝܢܝܢ
ܒܦܘܪ̈ܣܢܘܗܝ
ܕܗܠܝܢ
ܡܪ̈ܗܒܐ : ܐܟܐ
ܐܫܒܝܢܐ
ܕܝ ܒܬܪ
ܫܕ ܩܘܡ
f. 50 a ܡܚܝܬ : ܐܘܦ
ܗܘ ܣܒܐ
ܕܝ ܗܘܐ
ܪܡܐ ܟܠ
ܣܒܪܐ
ܕܣ̈ܗܕܐ :
ܕܠܐ ܗܘܬ
ܡܚܝܬܗ
ܒܢܫܐ ܣܓܝ :
ܘܗܘܐ

f. 55 b ܡܘܕܐ
ܠܐܠܗܐ
ܣܓܝ ܟܠ ܡܟܐ
ܕܐܬܟܒܫ
ܡܢܝܘܢ ܕܝ
ܗܘܐ ܕܠܐ
ܐܬܟܒܫ ܫܐܘܠ
ܒܫܘܠܡܗܘܢ
ܕܡܕܥܢܐ
ܕܐܬܦܠܓܘ :
ܘܗܘܐ ܒܟܐ
ܘܐܡܪ : ܘܝ
f. 50 a ܠܝ ܠܕܘܝܐ :
ܕܠܐ ܐܬܟܒܫܬ
ܫܐܘܠ
ܕܡܢܝܢܐ
ܕܐܒܗܬܐ
ܡܕܥܢܐ
ܕܐܬܦܠܓܘ
ܟܠ ܦܓܪܗ
ܕܡܫܝܚܐ :
ܗܕ

f. 55a ܘܗܘܬ ܕܝ
ܢܦܫܗܘܢ
ܡܢܛܪܘ *
ܘܗܘܝܢ
ܒܝܘܡܐ ܪܒܐ
ܡܒܪܢ ܐܘܢ
ܠܗܠܝܢ
ܕܐܬܦܠܓܘ
ܘܢܦܩܝܢ ܕܝ
ܠܗܠܝܢ ܐܬܪ̈ܢܐ
ܕܗܘܘ ܒܐܬ̈ܪܝܢ:
ܡܒܘ ܟܪ
f. 50b ܕܗܘܐ ܠܒܗ
ܕܒܝܬ ܘܠܐ
ܗܘܐ ܒܒܐ
ܘܡܬܐܒܠ
ܥܠ ܡܬܦܪ̈ܢܐ
ܘܒܢܝܫܐ
ܕܒܬܠܝܢ
ܒܐܣܟܡܐ
ܕܡܫܝܚܝܐ
ܘܡܫܝܚܘܬ

f. 55a ܕܠܐ ܪ̈ܚܡܝܐ
ܫܪܝܢ ܥܠ
ܐܪܒܥܐ: ܒܘܠ
ܚܕ ܘܚܕ
ܡܢܗܘܢ
ܡܠܘܐ: ܚܕ
ܪܫܗ ܡܢܩܒ:
ܘܚܪܢ ܡܢܩܒ
ܠܬܪ̈ܝܢ: ܚܪܢ
ܕܝ ܪܫܗ
ܥܠܝܗ ܠܬܪ̈ܝܢ:
ܡܢܐ ܠܝ ܒܪ
f. 50b ܕܐܬܗܦܟܬ ܥܠ
ܩܘܪܒܢܝܗܘܢ
ܕܡܫܡܫܬܐ
ܕܠܗܘ ܡܫܝܚܐ
ܕܠܐ ܪ̈ܚܡܝܢ
ܕܐܬܦܠܓܘ
ܐܒ̈ܗܝܢ
ܐܒ̈ܗܝܢ
ܘܫܒܩܝܢ ܗܘܘ
ܥܠ ܐܪܒܥܐ:

f. 30 b ܡܢ ܩܕ̈ܡ
ܠܗ ܡܘܫܐ
ܒܥܒܕܗ
ܕܐܠܗܐ ܀
ܡܛܠ ܕܝ
ܒܛܘܪܒ
ܟܠ ܗܠܝܢ
ܕܐܪܒܥܝܢ ܝܘܡܝܢ
ܘܒܨܘܪ̇ܒ ܀
ܘܐܪܒܥܝܢ
ܒܨܘܪ̇ ܀
ܘܟܠ ܗܠܝܢ
f. 27 a ܕܐܬ̈ܚܒܫܘ
ܩ̈ܕܡܝܢ
ܠܛܘܪܐ
ܩܕܝܫܐ ܀
ܘܡܛܠ ܐܘܦ
ܒܥܡܐ ܠܘܬ
ܘܒܕ ܡܫܝܚܕ
ܐܘܦ ܠܢ
ܗܘܘ ܡܛܠܝܢ ܀
ܠܟܕܘܠ ܕܠܐ

f. 30 b ܡܢ ܐܢܫ
ܠܘܩܒܠܗܘܢ ܀
ܐܠܐ ܐܠܗܐ
ܪܚܡܢܐ
ܗܘ ܕܦܐܫܛ
ܐܝܕܗ
ܠܡܥܕܪܘܬܐ
ܠܗܠܝܢ
ܕܩܕ̈ܡ ܠܗ
ܡܢ ܒܘܠܗ
ܠܒܗܘܢ ܀
ܘܦܩܕ
f. 27 a ܘܐܬܚܫܒܬ
ܥܠܐܒܝܬܐ
ܕܢܘܪܐ
ܒܪܝܫܗ
ܕܛܘܪܐ
ܩܕܝܫܐ ܀
ܘܗܘܬ
ܠܬܡܢ ܀
ܘܟܠܗ
ܛܘܪܐ

Two pages = one leaf of the ancient MS., are missing here.

ܪ̈ܚ⌜ܡܘ⌝ܬܐ f. 30 a
ܘܦܠܘ ܆ ܗܠܝܢ
ܕܝ ܕܗܘܘ
ܒܡܫܝ̈ܢ
ܒܐܬܪ̈ܝܢ
ܕܦܪ̈ܫܝܢ
ܒܪ ܫܡܫܘ
ܕܝ ܒܪܘܘ
ܠܚܝܠܐ ܚܕ.
ܦܪܢܣܐ ⌜ܚܡ⌝
ܡܢܒܪܝܗ
ܕܐܬܪܐ ܆
ܗܕܐ ܕܫܒܥܗ f. 27 b
ܕܠܘܩ ܆ ܗܡ
ܘܥܒܕ ܠܟ
ܒܒܢܗ
ܕܐܠܗܐ
ܗܘܐ ܆ ܩܠܝܐ
ܠܟ ܗܘܬ
ܡܫܡܘܢܝܬܗ
ܘܡܫܡܫܢܘܬܗ ܆
ܘܫܠܐ ܗܘܘ

ܢܡܫܚܐ f. 30 a
ܠܚܡ ܟܒ
ܡܢܒܪܝܗ
ܕܐܬܪܐ ܆
◯ܒܬܪ ܕܝ
ܢܡܫܚܐ
ܘܡ̈ܟܝܢ ܆ ܗܡ
ܥܠܝܐ ܢܚܠܘ
ܚܠܝܢ ܗܘܐ ܠܟ
ܕܗܪ̈ܘܡܐܝܢ ܆
ܠܒܝܬ
ܕܒܝܬܗ
ܘܒܢܝܐ ܡܟܢܬ f. 27 b
ܡܠܟܐ
ܕܗܪ̈ܘܡܝܢ ܗܘܐ
ܕܗܘܐ ܢܦܠ
ܡܢܒܪܐ ܆
ܗܠܝܢ ܕܝ
ܐܒܗܬܐ
ܕܐܬܪܬܫܘܐ
ܒܠܬܘܬܐ
ܕܗܘܐ ܢܚ

Two lines of the upper script have been erased in this leaf by the Arab owners of the MS. and with them some letters of the under script have also disappeared.

f. 58b ܘܡܫܠܡܝܢ
ܩܘܢܐ
ܕܚܕ ܒܫܘܒܐ :
ܘܒܦܘܪܐ
ܗܘܘ ܢܫܒܝܢ
ܙ̈ܘܓܐ ܡܙ̈ܝܢܐ :
ܦܘܓܪܗ
ܘܐܕܡܗ
ܕܡܪܐ
ܫܦܘܗ :
ܘܒܫܕܝܒܘ
ܗܘܘ ܐܘܠܝܢ
ܒܟܠ ܐܢܫ
f. 63a ܠܡܠܬܗ :
ܡܢܡܘܡܘܗܝ
ܕܝ ܐܘܒ
ܕܒܢܝܗܘܗܝ
ܗܘܝ ܕܡܠܟ̈ܝܢ
ܗܘܐ : ܘܗܘܘ
ܦܓܪܝܗܘܢ
ܩ̈ܘܡܝܢ
ܠܥܕܐ : ܗܝܟ

f. 58b ܕܐܠܗܘܪ
ܐܝܟ ܕܕܠܐ
ܦܓܪ ܗܘܘ :
ܠܐ ܓܪ ܗܘܘ
ܩܕܝܡ ܒܠܘܡ :
ܠܝ̈ܘܪܒܢܗ
ܕܦܓܪܐ :
ܠܐ ܚܡܪ :
ܘܠܐ ܡܢܚܝ :
ܘܠܐ ܠܚܡ :
ܒܦܪܝܢ ܗܘܐ
ܡܫܬܒܚ
ܠܗܘܢ : ܐܠܐ
f. 63a ܝܡܝܢܐ
ܬܘܡܪ̈ܝܢ
ܘܡܢܐ ܕܡܫܬܘܝ
ܠܗܘܢ :
ܠܒܥܠ ܕܝ
ܐܚܣܢܝܢ
ܕܐܬܝܢ ܕܢܬܠܘܢ
ܬܠܝܢ : ܗܘܐ
ܡܫܩܠ ܬܘܡ

Page 1 is on a missing leaf.

f. 58a ܐܫܬܘܝ ܠܐ
ܕܢܫܠܘܛ ܐܘܦ
ܒܐܬܪܐ
ܩܕܝܫܐ
ܕܡܕܒܪܐ
ܕܒܘܠܐ ܀
ܝܗܒܬ ܕܝ
ܒܪܗܣ
ܠܡܕܒܪܐ :
ܥܡ ܐܢܫܝܢ
ܕܫܠܝܢ ܡܢ
ܐܠܗܐ ܀
f. 63b ܕܗܘܘ ܐܪ̈ܠܝܢ
ܠܗܘܢ ܕܢ̈ܫܝܗܘܢ ܀
ܡܠܝܢ ܕܝ
ܠܗܘܢ ܒܢܦܫܗ
ܕܐܠܗܐ
ܠܬܡܢܬܥܣܪ
ܝܘ̈ܡܝܢ ܀
ܘܒܪ ܡܠܟܬ:
ܒܬܪܬ ܬܡܢ
ܡܢܝܢ

f. 58a ܘܝܘ̈ܡܝܢ ܀
ܡܬܒܣܡ
ܕܝ ܒܡܘܠܦܢܐ
ܕܠܗܘܢ
ܕܐܒܗܬܐ
ܘܩܕܝܫܝܐ
ܕܬܡܢ ܀
ܕܗܘܝܬ
ܡܢܝܢ ܐܝܠ
ܠܥܠܬܗܘܢ
ܠܒܪܠ
ܗܝܬܗ
f. 63b ܕܢܦܫܝ ܀
ܒܘܠܗ̇ ܠܪ̈
ܫܘܒܚܬܐ
ܡܬܝܗܒܝܢ
ܒܫܪܝܪܘܬܐ ܀
ܒܪ̈ܗܫܐ ܕܝ
ܕܫܘܒܚܬܐ
ܘܗܘ
ܡܬܒܠܥܝܢ
ܠܚܝܫܬܐ

THE FORTY MARTYRS OF THE SINAI DESERT

For EU product safety concerns, contact us at Calle de José Abascal, 56–1°, 28003 Madrid, Spain or eugpsr@cambridge.org.

www.ingramcontent.com/pod-product-compliance
Ingram Content Group UK Ltd.
Pitfield, Milton Keynes, MK11 3LW, UK
UKHW030902150625
459647UK00021B/2666

* 9 7 8 1 1 0 8 0 1 9 0 8 8 *